"Beware of *Dispatches from the Front* if you don't like being moved and inspired and shaken out of the ruts of your life. These are kingdom stories that build faith in the present providence of God over his mission and stir up action for the sake of lost and hurting people near and far. I would love to see thousands of people mobilized as senders and goers for the sake of the glory of Christ and the relief of suffering on the frontiers, especially eternal suffering."

John Piper, Founder, desiringGod.org; Chancellor, Bethlehem College and Seminary

"*Dispatches from the Front* is a thoughtful, moving, understated, and ultimately convicting narrative depicting the work of the gospel in some of the most challenging corners of the world. It tells of brothers and sisters in Christ who in God's grace display faithfulness and transcendent joy, unflagging zeal to share the gospel, and an unfettered allegiance to King Jesus. To read of the kingdom advance in the teeth of challenges is to learn humility and rekindle contrition, faith, and intercessory prayer."

D. A. Carson, Research Professor of New Testament, Trinity Evangelical Divinity School

"Like a war correspondent, Tim Keesee has brought us to the front—to walk down bomb-shattered streets, along jungle paths, and into the lives of our brothers and sisters in Christ. Their Christlike courage in living as 'lambs among wolves' is a striking witness to the power of the gospel."

Sen. Jim DeMint, President, The Heritage Foundation

"The Lord promised to call to himself people from every nation, tribe, and tongue, and few things thrill me more than seeing and hearing how he is fulfilling that promise. Tim Keesee has a remarkable ministry in traveling the world to seek out what the Lord is doing and to make these things known. *Dispatches from the Front* allows you to travel with him, and if you go along, you will be blessed, you will be encouraged, and you will praise God."

Tim Challies, blogger, Challies.com; author, *The Discipline of Spiritual Discernment*

"*Dispatches from the Front* is a fascinating look at how the gospel is penetrating some of the world's neediest places. These are regions where all the worst agonies of human life are multiplied and magnified relentlessly by war, extreme poverty, sex trafficking, drug dealing, false religion, and disease . . . but your spirit will be encouraged by the triumphant power of Christ."

Phil Johnson, Exec

D1364825

"We have been far more successful at westernizing the world than gospelizing it. Tim's book is a kind but firm challenge to a church that has exchanged the great commission for a smaller, more comfortable version. Each chapter is a serious wake-up call for churches and Christians to return to an authentic, New Testament mission."

Sam Horn, President, Central Theological Seminary

"This book is intriguing, well-written, and culturally informative, and it introduces us to fellow-believers who otherwise would remain unknown. Read it for those reasons. But read it first and foremost because it reveals anew the first-century Christ, who is now remaking diverse people of this twenty-first century into the elite citizens of his everlasting kingdom."

David J. Hesselgrave, Emeritus Professor of Mission, Trinity Evangelical Divinity School

"Riveting. Tim writes with artistry and passion about gospel needs and gospel triumphs. He labors in the world's toughest places and, through his journals, takes us along for the ride. Read this book. Rejoice. Weep. Pray. Then find a way to join those serving on the front lines for the glory of Jesus Christ."

Chris Anderson, Pastor, Killian Hill Baptist Church, Lilburn, Georgia

"*Dispatches from the Front* is a powerful book. It spreads a vision for God's mission to call a people for his name and provides incredible reminders of the gospel's power. Read it and your heart will be stirred to praise God for his mercy among the nations and to pray for its continued spread."

David M. Doran, President, Detroit Baptist Theological Seminary

DISPATCHES FROM THE FRONT

DISPATCHES
FROM THE
FRONT

STORIES OF GOSPEL ADVANCE IN
THE WORLD'S DIFFICULT PLACES

TIM KEESEE

FOREWORD BY JUSTIN TAYLOR

CROSSWAY

WHEATON, ILLINOIS

Library of Congress Cataloging-in-Publication Data
Keesee, Timothy.
  Dispatches from the front : stories of gospel advance in the world's difficult places / Tim Keesee ; foreword by Justin Taylor.
    pages cm
  Includes bibliographical references and index.
  ISBN 978-1-4335-4069-1 (tp)
  1. Missions. 2. Christianity—21st century. I. Title.
BV2061.3.K44   2014
270.8'3—dc23   2013037855

To my father
Carlton Eugene Keesee
(1934–2013)
a hero in the battle of life

Blessed are the eyes that see what you see! For I tell you that many prophets and kings desired to see what you see, and did not see it, and to hear what you hear, and did not hear it.

Luke 10:23–24

Little by little
One travels far.

J. R. R. Tolkien

CONTENTS

Foreword *by Justin Taylor*   11

Acknowledgments   15

Prologue: Danville, Virginia   17

1 End of Empire: The Former Soviet Republics   23

2 Children of Cain: The Balkans   49

3 Ten Sparrows: China   77

4 Within a Yard of Hell: Southeast Asia   101

5 Souls of the Brave: Bangladesh, India, and Pakistan   129

6 Amazing Grace: Liberia, Sierra Leone, and Guinea   159

7 Prison Break: The Horn of Africa and Egypt   181

8 Dimmed by Dust: Afghanistan and Iraq   209

Epilogue   235

Notes   237

FOREWORD

The apostle Paul, responding to criticism that he was putting himself forward and commending himself, acknowledged that he and his gospel coworkers—men and women on the frontlines of the advance of the kingdom—actually *do* "commend" themselves "in every way" (2 Cor. 6:4).

But how? What could he cite to demonstrate their missional integrity? What items make it on to their ministry résumé?

Explaining that they experienced the following with "great endurance," Paul paints a picture of what they have endured:

- afflictions
- hardships
- calamities
- beatings
- imprisonments
- riots
- labors
- sleepless nights
- hunger (2 Cor. 6:4–5).

Welcome to life on the frontlines.

But this isn't a Pauline pity party. He goes on to explain that in the upside-down, world-confounding kingdom, things are not as they seem. From a limited, worldly perspective, these workers on the frontlines look like losers. But in reality, they are men and women of whom the world is not worthy. Paul makes the contrast between how they are perceived and what they really are. They are treated:

- as impostors—and yet are true;
- as unknown—and yet well known;
- as dying—and behold, we live;
- as punished—and yet not killed;
- as sorrowful—yet always rejoicing;
- as poor—yet making many rich;
- as having nothing—yet possessing everything. (2 Cor. 6:8–10)

In particular, it's the phrase "sorrowful, yet always rejoicing" that comes to mind when I think of Tim Keesee and his ministry of visiting gospel workers on the front lines.

There's nothing fancy about the man. He's not famous. In fact, unless you've watched the Dispatches from the Front DVD series, you've probably never heard of him—and even if you have, you probably didn't catch his name. He's quiet and unassuming. He's humble and without guile. He's a faithful and ordinary man who serves an extraordinary God.

There's a certain world-weariness etched onto his face as he has spent years crisscrossing the globe, visiting and supporting and documenting the church around the world. But if you look closer, there is unmistakable joy. You can see it in the warmth of his smile and the twinkle of his eye and the welcome of his embrace as he greets a new brother and a new sister on the other side of the world and worships with yet another outpost of the global family of God. If the new heavens and the new earth will be filled with the redeemed from "every tribe and language and people and nation" (Rev. 5:9), then Tim Keesee has gotten a foretaste of the world to come.

In this book you will have a front-row seat to the most important work in history, as the great news of a bloody-sacrifice-turned-risen-King transforms lives around the world. You'll follow along with Tim's journeys over the past several years as he travels from the former Soviet Republics to the Balkans, from China to Southeast Asia, from Bangladesh, India, and Pakistan to Liberia, Sierra Leone, and Guinea, from the Horn of Africa to Egypt, from Afghanistan to Iraq. You'll see the joy and the sorrow, the pleasure and the pain, as he sees the glory of the gospel revealed afresh and yet still mourns the danger and bondage of soul-destroying sin.

Tim Keesee

No one will be reached with the gospel unless we *go* to them. Because no one will "hear without someone preaching" (Rom. 10:14), we must "go therefore and make disciples of all nations [Greek, *ethnē*, or people groups]" (Matt. 28:19). In order to do this, some of us are called to "*send* them on their journey in a manner worthy of God" (3 John 1:6). But whether you are a goer or a sender, none of us can see it all. We can only get a small glimpse of the kingdom based on where God has called us to serve. That is why I am excited for you to read this book. You can read it straight through or skip around according to your interests. But as you do, you will see the curtain pulled back on the glorious and unstoppable advance of the gospel. This is a dangerous book to read, for you may never be the same.

Come and see.

Justin Taylor

ACKNOWLEDGMENTS

Many people have helped me along the path that wends its way through the pages of this book. I am so grateful for friends whose mentoring and interpreting have guided me on this journey. For Jan Tolwinski of Warsaw, who first showed me the way when the Iron Curtain was parting. For Misko Horvatek of Croatia—his courageous compassion during the war modeled risk-taking gospel ministry for me; along bomb-shattered roads he always had a talent for finding a good cappuccino in a war zone! For David Hosaflook, pioneer missionary to Albania, my friend, my brother, my hero. For Natasha Vins—her experiences and those of other believers during the Soviet persecution were cross-shaped; she regaled me with many of their stories on long train rides across Russia. For Paul Choo of Singapore—his vision for unreached fields have lifted the eyes of many, including mine. For JD Crowley—who first showed me that Christ's kingdom has no borders.

There are others whose acts of kindness kept me going. Their names cannot be published here, but they are written in the Lamb's book. Though they were surely aware they were not entertaining an angel unawares, they showed generous hospitality to this stranger by providing a refuge for the night or helping me get on the right train or introducing me to my brothers and sisters meeting in secret.

Closer to home, I am indebted to the entire Frontline team, who have cheered me on and prayed me on—especially John Hutcheson, Steve Leatherwood, and Al Carper, steadfast friends since the first days of Frontline Missions. I am grateful, too, to Pete Hansen. His skillful videography has added color and voice to many of these kingdom stories through the Dispatches from the Front DVD series. For Allan Sherer, who is another Epaphroditus, "my brother and fellow worker and fellow soldier . . . and minister to my need" (Phil. 2:25). I am also grateful to Senator Jim DeMint for the doors he has encouraged me to walk through. As his star has risen, the compass of his life has remained fixed—centered in the truth of his life's verse: "For freedom Christ has set us free" (Gal. 5:1).

Justin Taylor at Crossway has been a Barnabas to me since the day this book was conceived. Justin has an enormous capacity for work matched with an enormous capacity for kindness. He is truly a gift of grace to the church and to me personally. Special thanks also to Tara Davis—editor extraordinaire—who was a joy to work with!

Special thanks to my daughter and son, Sarah and Tim, who grew up with their passports handy. Their companionship has brought me great joy as we shared many journeys and adventures together. My wife, Debbie, has been my dependable friend and in-dispensable partner during all these years and miles of ministry. And as is her gift, Debbie brought order out of the chaos of a dozen or more journals scribbled across four continents and turned them into a working manuscript. Her love for me has been more evidence of God's love for me. Though our life together has often meant life apart from each other—together we share in this adventure of fol-lowing Christ and the joy of finding treasure in unreached fields.

PROLOGUE

DANVILLE, VIRGINIA

A train calls to me in the night silence. For as long as I can remember, it has provided the music—and my pen the words—to a restless life. A million miles later, I'm back where I grew up—and the train's whistle is as sweet and lonely as ever. Outside my window, a half-moon lays its light over the contours of the backyard. I can still trace the lines of our old ball field. Actually, moonlight isn't needed. I can see and hear it best with my eyes closed: It's another summer night long ago—fireflies swirl in a ballet of light, and the game goes on until it's too dark to see.

Just down the road is the place where I stood beneath a star-filled sky much like tonight and knew that Christ had forgiven all my sins. I felt the rush of freedom like a pardoned prisoner who suddenly finds that not only has his name been cleared, but he has been loaded with titles of honor—beloved, heir, son.

Here in my old room, Mama used to play hymns on a beaten-up piano with a keyboard that looked like an ugly grin—its ivories yellowed, cracked, or missing. I remember how pretty she was at the piano. She had a lilting style that made me sing, even when I was too young to read. An old plaque still hangs on the living room wall: "The way of the Cross leads home." Mama has finished that journey, and yet tonight on this side, amid a clutter of memories and the mocking monotony of a ticking clock, I miss her.

One of the things I love her for is that she gave me to the Lord—which meant that she had to let me go. Travel just wasn't in our family's DNA. Our roots run deep in the red clay of the Virginia foothills. Only things like world wars and great depressions could move us away, but always we came back to these familiar hills. I was the first in ten generations to leave Virginia. So even though Mama did not understand my wanderlust, like Hannah, she had given her son to the Lord, and she kept her word, even when it hurt. She bought a globe—it's still here on the dresser—and over the years, she traced the paths of her promise.

And so, I've gone far from this place. A sixteen-year-old sailor who used to be me looks down from the shelf. The picture is faded, but I still smell the salt. Back then, my small world suddenly became as vast as the ocean. And everything I saw I wrote about, filling in the blanks that only imagination could attempt before.

My path wound on. For a while I took up writing textbooks, and then teaching, but I escaped my cubicle and classroom to help pastors in Eastern Europe, as the winds of freedom began to stir in persecuted churches as well as in these prison states. Browsing them now, my journals seem to read like the pages of the history of our times. I witnessed the pullout of Soviet troops and tanks in Poland, stood at the barricades in Vilnius with Lithuanian patriots, and walked through the fresh rubble of the Berlin Wall. Once Soviet Communism fell, the pieces could never quite be put together again. Freedom unleashed forces of both war and peace, so there were times in the new Russia's first springtime when everything seemed possible, and there were times in Bosnia during the last winter of the war when everything seemed hopeless.

With the dissolution of the Soviet Empire, I witnessed the fall of one great power and the rise of another. China was stirring and stretching, her influence evident far beyond her soaring cities. I saw it from the backwaters of Laos and Vietnam to the diamond fields of Sierra Leone in West Africa. At the same time my travels in Asia and Africa brought me face to face with another force—violent Islam.

The horizons of my world were changing, but in an unexpected way. It had less to do with passport stamps and frequent flyer miles than it did with my own heart. Growing up, when I thought about the church around the world, it looked like my church. That was all I knew. Sure, Christians in other countries had different languages and cultures, but if their worship styles were different or their theological preferences deficient, well, that's why I was going over to teach them. And so, as is too often the case in missions, church planting resembles church franchising instead.

However, it was soon evident that I had more to learn than to teach. What I learned wasn't just a crash course in Cultural Appreciation 101, although I did learn to adapt—whether using chopsticks, tying my own turban, or eating bamboo worms. What I really learned was more of the gospel in all its dimensions—its height and depth and extent as I saw it cross every kind of barrier to save souls. The cultural differences in the church only displayed the truth that "by your blood you ransomed people for God from every tribe and language and people and nation" (Rev. 5:9).

I have seen empires come and go, but never have I seen anything so radical and pervasive as the gospel of the kingdom. The kingdom of Christ is diverse yet unified, boundless yet bound; for our lives are forever bound up in his life—and thus bound up with all other believers. We are like family, his body. The more I grasped the gospel, the more I loved Christ—and the more I loved him, the more I loved his people. I found a certain likeness in them.

In difficult places I have met brothers and sisters living like lambs among wolves. They seem to have stepped right out of Hebrews 11 because "some were tortured, refusing to accept release, so that they might rise again to a better life. Others suffered mocking and flogging, and even chains and imprisonment" (Heb. 11:35–36). They are my friends, my teachers, my heroes. Yet the gospel gives me perspective not to think that the greatest Christians are *over there*; neither are the greatest Christians *over here*. Actually, Christ is the greatest, and in every land he is saving, calling, and enabling men and women to take risks to advance his kingdom—cross-bearers who love him more than their stuff, even more than their own lives.

These are the foot soldiers of gospel advance, and I love to walk point with them and write their stories. I share Ernie Pyle's affection for those at the front in every danger and season. Pyle, the legendary combat journalist of World War II, wrote, "I love the infantry because they are the underdogs. They are the mud-rain-frost-and-wind boys. They have no comforts, and they even learn to live without the necessities. And in the end they are the guys that wars can't be won without."[1]

On the gospel front as well—one that also has its share of real bullets and bombs—it's the foot soldiers that God uses to move the boundaries of his kingdom into more and more hearts. Not long ago I was on the Syrian border where Christians run a little clinic, providing medical services along with the gospel to Bedouin tribes. A British nurse named Claire told me that radical Muslims have threatened to kill them and burn the hospital down. She also told me they had not reported these threats because the government would close the clinic for the safety of the staff. She said matter-of-factly, "Whether it's the bad man with the gun or the nice man with the tie, the result is the same—the clinic will be closed. We have no reason to stop now. They have stolen our vehicles and threatened to kill us, but they have not harmed us yet and cannot unless God permits it—and even then, it will be OK because we will be with the Lord." Even though she had faced armed robbers and lethal force, Claire's voice was as steady as her faith. Claire doesn't have a death wish; she has a living hope. She knows Christ is powerful to save her—and to save all who come to him.

A million miles lie between me and this room where I spent my childhood. Here I dreamed of the world beyond my view. I could never have imagined that the world I wanted to explore was just a window to my King's saving work. The following are the stories of kingdom advance—dispatches written along the way, often scribbled in the moment, praising our Captain's brilliance, describing his victories, and telling of his gracious, sleepless care as he walks among us on the front lines.

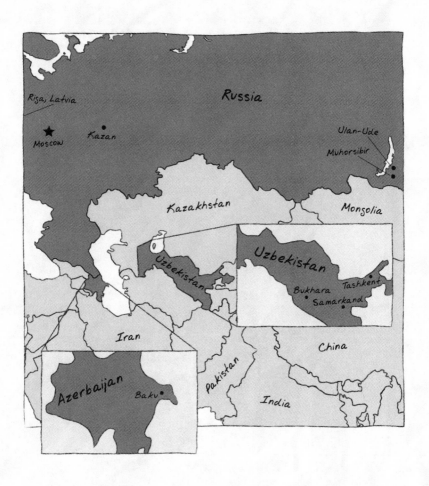

/
END OF EMPIRE

The Former Soviet Republics

Capitalism meets Communism: selling old Soviet banners at a street market in Kiev, Ukraine

It's easy to romanticize the experiences of the underground church in the Soviet Union: cool, courageous stories of smuggling Bibles; cat-and-mouse games with the KGB; and images of Soviet Christians worshiping in the forest, their pews fallen logs and their chapel walls silver birch with a cathedral ceiling that reached the sky. But it was no picnic, no James Bond movie. The Soviet Christians were brutally persecuted, and their pastors' preparation for ministry usually took place in a prison rather than a seminary.

But the underground church was not underground. Believers spoke of Christ and won many to him, even in prison. This was

Galina's story. Galina Vilchinskaya was a twenty-three-year-old Sunday school teacher who spent five years in prison for her gospel work; but prison, hunger, and beatings could not silence her. She led many in her prison to the Lord, so she was transferred to another prison—and after that, yet another. For her, these transfers were just new gospel opportunities. Finally, Galina was transported by prison train to the utter east of Siberia, along with scores of other prisoners—the worst of the worst. As the condemned in their cages rumbled on through the Siberian vastness, the din of cursing and fighting was broken by a clear, sweet voice of singing. It was Galina singing of her Savior. A hush fell over the train car. Even the most hardened criminals turned their faces away to hide their tears—and mile after mile, hymn after hymn, Galina sang the gospel.[1]

It's really absurd, though, that the full force of the Soviet Union was bent on crushing a Sunday school teacher for the crime of "being a Sunday School teacher." Such senseless hatred, when it erupts to the surface, is like opening a furnace door to hell. But the gates of hell were no match for Galina's God. One striking proof of that is that today Galina is a pastor's wife in Siberia, where once she was a prisoner of an empire that no longer exists.

The collapse of the Soviet state brought unprecedented freedom and gospel opportunity to believers living across the eleven time zones of that massive empire. Fifteen new countries rose up from the rubble—and new tyrants rose up, too. Persecution has returned—but now, it's not only from tyrannical governments but also from resurgent Islam, over a vast swath of central Asia, from the Caspian Sea to Kazakhstan.

The rise and crash of nations provides a perfect backdrop for our Christ's unending kingdom and his saving grace—news so good that even a starving prisoner couldn't help but sing of it! Christians in these unshackled lands are still singing of Jesus, still speaking of him.

RIGA, LATVIA

This afternoon Sergei and Ilona, friends of mine from Warsaw, drove me to the outskirts of Riga. There along the shores of the

Daugava, the old Soviet naval base and airfields sit in quiet decay. Once the proud vanguard of a great empire, the sprawling military complex is succumbing to the ravages of rust and crabgrass. Yet many retired veterans still live in the crumbling apartments near the base, and that is what took me there today—to look up an old friend. I've been here before—a dozen years ago. Then it was a blustery night with a light dusting of snow. A friend of mine arranged for me to stay with a Christian, and so I was brought here. Nothing looked familiar today, though, until the door of apartment 38 opened up, and there was Alexei Beloborodov. He was a bit grayer, but still ramrod straight with a soldier's bearing, and he was as kind as ever. Twelve years ago he took a stranger in on a cold night. I remember he made me a meal of black bread and fried eggs with steaming black tea. It was right after the USSR collapsed, and the ruble was worthless. I learned later that my host was so poor that he only ate one meal a day at that time, but his little one-room apartment was a place of joy and hospitality.

How good it was to see Brother Alexei again today! He invited us to tea. There have been so many questions I have wanted to ask him about his life, and today was my chance. Alexei went to war at age sixteen—that was in 1943. As a young tank commander, he quickly proved himself in battle, as evidenced by the box of medals he brought out of his closet and by his scars. He fought all the way to the smoldering ruins of Hitler's Berlin. He returned home in victory, only to find he had no home. His village near Moscow had been destroyed in the war and his family all killed or scattered. So Alexei returned to the only life he knew—the Soviet military. He became a naval intelligence officer, got married, raised children, and spent nearly thirty years in the service.

As an officer, Alexei had access to shortwave radio, and he heard Christian broadcasts beamed into the Soviet Union. The gospel changed him forever! He repented of his sins and received Christ into his life. That was 1968. He had no Bible, no church, no pastor, no Christian friend—no one to fellowship with, except the Lord.

Alexei told me that he would often take long walks deep into the woods, where he would pray and weep and sing. His was a lonely walk. It was seven years before he met another Christian—after he left the military. He said when he first learned the man was a Christian, Alexei gave him a big bear hug before he could even get the words out to the surprised man!

Yet Alexei's walk would get even lonelier. Shortly afterward, he was baptized, and this public testimony of his faith was a great dividing line in his life. His wife divorced him, and his children would have nothing to do with him. For several years he was homeless, living in a cold, dank basement without electricity or running water. He eventually found a job in a factory and a place to stay, but his penchant for passing out smuggled tracts and sharing his faith kept him in trouble with the KGB during the years of persecution.

For over twenty-five years now—during persecution and during freedom—Alexei has never missed church a single time. In fact, when he worked at the factory and was scheduled to work on Sunday, he would pay a coworker a full day's wage to take his place!

We talked until dusk, and he took out a little box of mementos. Among them were yellowing photographs of a handsome, young officer in his crisp uniform, decorated with many medals. He took one of them out of the box. Stamped in red on dull silver were the Russian words—"for bravery in battle." He gave it to me, but I said, "I cannot take this—it is a treasure won at great cost." He smiled and said, "I am going home soon and will have no need of it there."

My friend has known so much loneliness in his life, and yet the Lord has filled the emptiness with himself. We walked outside, prayed together, and parted ways. As I set out for Riga, the last, long light of day brightened the birches as old Brother Beloborodov turned and walked back alone.

ON THE RAIL, MOSCOW TO KAZAN, RUSSIA

The Kazan Express jostled out of the dusty Moscow rail station and lurched eastward, slipping through a sprawling, industrial section of the city cast in hues of concrete gray and rusty red. Outside of Moscow, though, even with approaching twilight, there was vibrant color—a spring countryside waking from the long Russian winter—dappled forests of birch, fresh green fields, and little cherry orchards wreathed with white blossoms. Despite the unseasonable heat, Pavlo, my friend and interpreter from Kiev, fills the teapot a second time. I enjoy another strong, steaming cup as we settle in for the evening and our five-hundred-mile trek to the east.

KAZAN, RUSSIA

After a long night on the train, I awoke to see the morning sun shimmering on the vast Volga River. Thin light fingered through birches and maples dressed in the crayon colors of spring. Mist hung over the vast swath of the great river, leaving the minarets of the White Kremlin in silhouette on the sunrise side of the city.

I think my heart skipped a beat at first sighting this storied shore. The legendary city of the Golden Horde was Ivan the Terrible's prized conquest, the gateway to Siberia and an even greater empire. But I had little time to relive the past, for as soon as we stepped off the train, we were stuffed into a little Lada and went careening through the streets of Kazan with Pastor Mikhail Trofimov. He drives like Jehu, but it was well that he did, for we barely made it in time for the Sunday service, where I joined the slate of preachers. Typically, there are two or three sermons in a service, punctuated with hymns, prayer, and poetry. The morning service concluded around noon with the afternoon service following at 1:30. This proximity is necessary, since few people have vehicles; the distances to walk and the cost of train tickets make it best to have the two services before and after lunch.

Between services I got better acquainted with Pastor Mikhail over a flavorful lunch of pickle soup, smoked sardines, and buttermilk. Pastor is an intense and energetic man whom God is greatly using here in the Kazan region. Because of his commitment to a trained ministry, he has organized a two-week Bible school. I'm teaching Pastoral Epistles starting in the morning.

KAZAN, RUSSIA

We have a good group of students at our Bible school, which is meeting in a borrowed classroom of a public school. Despite the fact that they have seven hours of instruction each day, they are attentive and diligent. We had expected about twenty students, but as of today we have thirty-three. Most of them are pastors who, during the years of persecution, never had the opportunity for formal Bible training. Some of the pastors have traveled considerable distances to be here, even from as far as the city of Perm—a seventeen-hour train trip to Kazan.

Lectured this morning, and in the afternoon accompanied Pastor Gennady Yeliazarov of Kazan to appeal to the commandant over all the prisons in Tatarstan to allow us into the strict-regime prison on the west bank of the Volga. Gennady also hoped to gain greater concessions for his ministry among prisoners, such as having Communion for believers and baptizing new converts.

Gennady, who serves as one of the pastors here, has a great heart for prisoners, for he was once a prisoner himself. His crime? Preaching the gospel and organizing choirs in various parts of the Soviet Union. When the KGB caught up with him, he was in Uzbekistan, training choirs among the underground churches there. Gennady was sent to prison in Rostov near the Black Sea. Each cell in his gulag held a hundred and fifty men with barely enough room for all to stand. The only facilities was a bucket in each cell. When Gennady first arrived, the guard took him to his cell. When he opened the door, it was so packed with standing prisoners that Gennady said, "There is no room here." The guard then shoved him in with a laugh saying, "Then make room," and slammed the door. Gennady spent three years in this gulag for the cause of Christ.

The irony of our meeting today was that the commandant was once the police chief in Gennady's village. He was the man who had ransacked Gennady's home looking for Bibles. He was the one who had hounded the pastor and his family and flock. He was the man who had gathered evidence against Gennady for which he was ultimately sent to prison. Now, after all these years had passed, they met again—the preacher and the persecutor.

There was no animosity from Gennady. None. In fact, he had told me earlier that going to prison had been a "good thing." I was puzzled and asked, "How was it a good thing?" "If I had never gone to prison," he replied, "then I would not have been able to understand prisoners and reach them with the gospel. The Lord has allowed me to lead thirty prisoners to Christ already." In fact, that is why we were meeting the commandant. It would take special permission for these men to be baptized and receive the Lord's Supper inside the Soviet-style prison. Only the commandant could give such permission. Actually, Gennady had already gone "over his head" in asking permission, because he had requested it of the Lord in prayer.

Pastor Gennady: "Slava Bogu!"

As is typical with these ex-Communist encounters, our meeting with the commandant turned out to be a long wait, interrupted occasionally by promises of a meeting. During the wait, we walked around Lenin University, named for Kazan's most famous dropout; the impatient revolutionary studied here for only three months. Afterward, Gennady and I returned to the prison headquarters. When we were finally given admittance, we climbed many flights of stairs, and, after more waiting, we were at last escorted into the commandant's office. There he sat behind a desk with so many telephones on it that I thought he must collect them. Behind his darkened glasses was a hard, oily face. He and Gennady entered into a sometimes intense discussion that lasted for nearly an hour. I had little to do at the meeting, other than the fact that Gennady believed having an American "doctor" present would help the cause of gaining concessions.

At the end of the meeting, we all shook hands and were escorted out. The discussion had been in rapid-fire Russian, so I didn't know what the outcome was until we walked away and Gennady leaned over and whispered, *"Slava Bogu"* (Glory to God)! God, by his grace and sovereignty, turned the commandant's flinty heart. He agreed that we can preach in the strict-regime prison tomorrow night, and my brother Gennady may hold baptismal services there and strengthen believers around the Lord's Table. I agree with Gennady—*Slava Bogu!*

KAZAN, RUSSIA

After lectures today, Gennady, Pavlo, and I took the train out to the strict-regime prison, where two thousand murderers, kidnappers, and assorted thieves and rapists are packed in behind steel bars and razor wire. Among these criminals were those who had accepted the Savior, the "Friend of Sinners." Many of these men came to the service, and I believe our visit encouraged them in the Lord.

To reach the meeting place, we had to surrender our passports, receive warnings about assaults, and go through three steel doors with our escort. Then we proceeded through a maze of cordoned walkways in the prison yard. The men crowded on both sides of us, their faces dark, eyes empty, forms shrunken. This is a maximum security prison, and, unlike its American counterpart, there is no cable TV or air-conditioned fitness center.

It was a privilege to have a service with these prisoners. About thirty gathered, of which about twenty-five are professing believers. We had hymns accompanied by a guitar. I preached, and Pavlo interpreted. There was good attention and many expressions of gratitude from the prisoners before the guards escorted us out. Surprisingly, the officer in charge stayed for the service. He, too, thanked us for coming and even invited us back! We returned by train to Kazan with much joy, recalling Isaiah's words, "The Spirit of the Lord GOD is upon me, because the LORD has anointed me to bring good news to the poor; he has sent me to bind up the broken-hearted, to proclaim liberty to the captives, and the opening of the prison to those who are bound" (Isa. 61:1).

KAZAN, RUSSIA

Spent much of the day in the city. Gennady took us all around Kazan. As far back as the Mongols, Kazan has been an important crossroad between East and West. It developed into an important industrial center during World War II, as strategic industry was moved further east, away from the German offensive. In order to supply the resistance, munitions production and aircraft design were done here. Today, much of the state industries are crumbling, casualties of perestroika. There is one massive plastics factory on the outskirts of Kazan. It is a sprawling, black-plumed complex, belching fumes into the air night and day. Some of the smokestacks look like giant Roman candles, as gas fires lit at the top burn off the most noxious pollutants.

In the heart of the city, amid the confluence of the Kazanka and Volga Rivers, sits the White Kremlin, a citadel that dates back to the time of the Golden Horde. All around the kremlin, the mosques and orthodox churches reflect the religious and cultural divide between Tatar and Russian. We entered one mosque, and the imam proudly showed us everything—from the pulpit to the washrooms, where men ceremoniously purify themselves in preparation for prayer.

One of the great needs in reaching Tatar Muslims with the gospel is to have the Bible and tracts published in the Tatar language. A century ago, the Gospels and Psalms were published in Tatar, but more needs to be done to effectively reach these six million Tatars!

After visiting the Volga River port, we returned to the apartment to prepare for this evening's Bible study. When Pastor Mikhail introduced me, I was delighted that he did so with a title of acceptance and respect by calling me by my patronymic name: "Timothy Carlovitch" (Timothy, son of Carl). I spoke on the subject of the resurrection of Jesus Christ, making a careful exposition of the theme. I was struck by the attention of these people, who sat for an hour on pine board benches and listened closely. Afterward, I returned to a believer's home for supper. Viktor and his wife Lyda prepared a fine meal. When our evening together was drawing to a close, they asked me to tell a story to their eight children, one that would help them learn not to fight and quarrel among themselves. I wasn't sure how to fill such a tall order, but suddenly I remembered the story of "The King and the Hawk." It was fun to see their wide-eyed expressions as I dramatized this old tale about Genghis Khan, who ruled their world long ago . . . and who also seemed to have problems with his temper.[2]

KAZAN, RUSSIA

Preached this morning from the little book of Philemon, emphasizing God's love to the least and how we must see people as individuals, winning them to Christ one by one. There must have been one hundred and fifty people packed into the room, with many standing along the walls. It was a good service with wonderful singing, especially the choir, who sang the Nicene Creed in Russian. During the service, two people came forward in repentance and profession of

Christ. One was an old woman who for years had sought satisfaction in the dead rituals of Russian Orthodoxy but found none. This morning she lifted her voice in confession and thanksgiving to the Savior. A young man also came forward in repentance. His troubled life has been weighed down with the added guilt from his years in the Soviet Army, fighting in Afghanistan. I believe this morning God brought peace to his war-torn soul.

After a quick lunch, Pastor and I walked to the town center for an evangelistic meeting, with Pavlo interpreting. One town official, an old Communist still wearing his Soviet badge, came to the meeting and listened attentively. Three raised their hands, expressing their need for Christ, and Pastor Mikhail counseled with them afterward. It is interesting to see the older people getting saved. Younger people have been so thoroughly indoctrinated with atheism that they must first come to a basic knowledge of God. However, the older generation heard of God in their youth. Now, despite many years under Communism, they have a spiritual hunger to know this God personally.

Late tonight, Mikhail arranged for me to meet his friend, Tahir. Tahir is a converted Tatar Muslim who was raised in Tashkent, Uzbekistan. As a young man, he was led to Christ through the example and witness of believers in Latvia. His heart is for winning his people—Muslims—to Christ. In Tahir's words, "You must reach Muslims with the language of love." Then, with his quick smile, he added, "Even a dog responds to that language." And Muslims are responding to the love of Jesus Christ, as demonstrated through this quiet, courageous evangelist. Tahir has already planted two churches in the Kazan region, which are now pastored by men he won to Christ and discipled. He is now planting a third church; however, like the apostle Paul, "a wide door for effective work has opened" to Tahir, but "there are many adversaries" (1 Cor. 16:9). He has received violent threats from Muslims and Russian Orthodox leaders, and now the KGB has given him orders to leave Kazan within the month. He has already moved his family—his wife and four children—and he will soon join them. For now, he is trying to shepherd his little flock and discern what to do next.

Tahir is brokenhearted over being torn from his people, yet I don't think this is the end. The imams, in league with the KGB, may think they are through with Tahir—but God isn't through with him. There is one thing that Tahir said to me tonight that still sticks in my mind and heart like a thorn of truth. Comparing the response to the gospel by Muslims he has reached with the indifference and fear of Christians to speak of the Savior, he said, "The world is more willing to receive the gospel than Christians are willing to give the gospel."

ON THE RAIL TO MOSCOW

My last day in Kazan. The weather turned cold, and the students arrived for morning lectures bundled against the chill wind. After the morning session, we all gathered at the Yeliazarovs for a final meal together. There were hymn-singing and special testimonies of how the Lord had worked in lives through our time together. One man, old Pavel Mayorov, stood with tears in his eyes and said the study had brought him back to a love for the Book. Afterward, Brother Mayorov asked to meet with me. I knew that he had been a tank gunner, an officer in the Soviet Army. He was thrice-wounded in fierce battles against the Germans. Shrapnel scars on his neck and the large shrapnel still lodged in his hand witnessed to his being in the thick of the fight.

Pavel Mayorov is Chuvash. His father, Sergei, was the first Chuvash to become a Christian in this remote and fiercely independent region of central Russia. He was converted through the ministry of the Salvation Army in 1911. At the time, Sergei was stationed in Finland in the Czar's Army, but he joined this "army" too, playing the horn and mandolin and sharing his faith in evangelistic meetings. Later as a preacher and gifted musician, he brought the gospel to this land and his people.

Sergei's son, Pavel, was born in 1922 but didn't embrace the faith of his father until 1977. By then he had retired as an officer in the Soviet Army and was a leading Communist Party member in Tatarstan. His wife and children had come to Christ, and despite his opposition, he could not deny the change in their lives. Finally, he went to a house meeting of underground believers to see and hear for himself.

He told me that when he heard the gospel preached, he was so overcome with its power that he said to himself, "I must resist this . . . I must leave or I will not be able to resist." He got up to leave, but there were so many crowded into the room that he couldn't get out. He sat down again and tears and prayers came forth. He said, "I do not know how the words came, for I had never prayed before; but I cried out to God, and he saved me." Tears still welled up as the old man recalled with joy the day he came to the Savior.

With informants all around, and given his status in the party, the KGB was quick to pick him up for interrogation. This was just the beginning of ten years of harassment and persecution as Pavel Mayorov identified with God's people. He lost his high position and a good income, but he had won Christ—and the old warrior never looked back.

One surprising, parting blessing this afternoon was that Gennady became a grandpa again. His son Andre and daughter-in-law Luba had a son whom they named Timothy, after me. Andre promised to send me a picture of my namesake.

Tonight many from the church gathered on the train platform to bid us farewell as we set out for Moscow. There were hymn-singing, prayers, and embraces as we reluctantly parted ways. They were still singing and waving as we slipped away from the station. Their voices were soon lost to the distance and their faces to the dusk, as my train wends westward, pursuing the fleeting tints of the day.

IN FLIGHT TO ÜLAN ÜDE, RUSSIA

Pavlo and I flew from Moscow to Irkutsk—deep in Siberia—and are now in a vintage prop plane to Ülan Üde. The carpet is worn down to the plywood floor, and our seats are crumbling sponge with threadbare covers. The air is thick and sweaty. This flight is not luxurious, but it is cheap and fast—merely sixteen dollars for the forty-five-minute flight (versus twenty-five dollars for a ten-hour train ride). The view from here is better, too. The endless green taiga forest suddenly plunges into the boundless blue Baikal. Along the eastern shore at Kadane, there is a strange frozen delta, a slurry of brown ice and spring green, laced with rivers and rivulets feeding the great lake.

We are flying over Buryatia. Buryats are Mongols living in Russia. There are perhaps a million of them—most of them concentrated here near the Mongolian border. Beneath us, little villages dot the landscape, and from our altitude some are clearly arranged in circles, reminiscent of the old encampments of the mighty Khans.

LATE NIGHT, MUHORŜIBIR, RUSSIA

I'm sleeping tonight on the porch of the home of Vasily and Seraphima Udintsev, a village house at 4 Communist Street, Muhorŝibir, in the Russian Republic of Buryatia, somewhere north of outer Mongolia. The Siberian summer gets quite cool in the evening, and so I am bundled up for bed tonight. A few lines about today . . .

The drive from Ülan Üde provided us with a good glimpse of Buryatia. The villages and towns look like frontier settlements with small log houses and stockade-like fences enclosing their gardens and corrals. It is a rich and remote land. The road follows the Selenga River, which flows up from Mongolia. It curves its way through a green valley, where sturdy Mongol youths herd cattle and black hawks loft in the wind. Our Buryat taxi driver stopped the car, and we climbed a little ridge for a better view.

This raw, pristine beauty, though, masks a hard and unforgiving land. Winters can get to -50° here. It's now June 7, and I noticed remnants of ice that are still three feet thick near the river. A family's survival depends on what their gardens yield and what their cows, pigs, and goats can contribute. With just two and a half months of frost-free days, life is intense, and words like "harvest" and "survival" are synonymous.

Such hardness and remoteness made this an excellent place to exile men of faith. One of those men was Vasily Udintsev, my host here. A pastor in Gorky and a skilled mechanic, he spent five years underground, cobbling together printing equipment for the secret presses that turned out copies of the Bible. For this crime, he was sentenced to five years in prison here. Like sparks from a fire, he and his dear wife Seraphima were cast into this distant corner, and ever since, they have brought light to those who sat in darkness.

About midnight tonight I went to find the outhouse. Along the way, I found Seraphima at the edge of the field. The only light was from a little fire with which she was boiling some gray goop, and then ladling the steaming gruel into a kettle of dandelions and wild greens. She was stirring this stew and filling buckets with it. I really didn't know what she was doing—maybe making breakfast for the morning, I thought! We couldn't communicate, but I had a flashlight to find the path and helped carry the buckets for her. She led me to the pigpen, and then I happily realized this was not my breakfast, but rather the pigs' supper. They seemed equally pleased! We worked at this for about a half hour and have just come in. Days are long and nights short here. The labor of living demands it.

A big yellow moon rises over Mongolia, and I think of my home so far away. Pavlo said to me today, "Now we are really in the middle of nowhere," and so we are. So goodnight from nowhere.

MUHORSIBIR, RUSSIA

Had open-air meetings in the market this morning. The young people of the church—Sasha, Natasha, Zhenna, and Tanja—set up a table with Bibles and gospel tracts. They sang and recited poetry, and Pavlo and I preached. The gatherings were small, but still we were able to share the Word of Life with several folks. Two in particular showed great concern for their souls and promised to come to the Sunday service.

Tonight we had a preaching service and examination of baptismal candidates that lasted four hours. During that time, a violent windstorm struck, knocking out power and stripping branches from trees. The lights went out and the shutters banged, but we carried on.

Had a late supper. Seraphima's supper table is always filled with discoveries—most of them pleasant. There were mushrooms from the forest and greens from the field in the soup, salted fish from Baikal, potatoes and onions from the garden, wild currants from the mountains—they all found their way here. Young women and boys gathered just beyond the doorway to watch and to listen to talk of faraway places, of an outside world.

MUHORŜIBIR, RUSSIA

The Lord's Day. The baptismal service, despite the wind and rain, was held at a lake near Muhorŝibir. We walked about two miles down the main road and then another two miles to reach the lake. Much of the path was through a forest of paper white birch. Along the way, folks picked bouquets of wildflowers for those being baptized. The flowers were strange to me—but very beautiful. There was a brilliant orange one called *zharkee,* found only in Siberia. *Zharkee* means "little flames" and is well named. There were also wild roses called *shepovnyk* and bundles of bluebells.

Three believers were baptized: Ana, an older lady of sweet disposition; a young man named Sasha; and Tanja, a young Buryat lady. Tanja and her mother had abandoned the empty rituals of Buddhism and found life and meaning in Christ. Tanja's hair is like black silk and nearly reaches her knees. She tied the tresses up and, in the face of a cold, driving rain, walked barefoot into the Siberian lake to join her pastor. She never flinched, but it made me shiver just thinking about it! Afterward we all gathered on the bank, and Russian voices lifted in song—"Happy day, happy day, when Jesus washed my sins away."

There is only one little car among all the church members. While it shuttled people back to the church, the rest of us began walking until it was our turn. I preferred to walk than wait, and so I covered another four miles back to the church, where in the late afternoon, a Communion service was held. I preached from John 1—the same message that John the Baptist preached after a baptismal service: "Behold, the Lamb of God!"

The service today started at ten in the morning and lasted over seven hours. It has been a good day but a long one, and I'm beginning to wonder why I'm still up scribbling, for I can hardly raise my pen.

ÜLAN ÜDE, RUSSIA

Our last night in Buryatia. It is eleven o'clock, and it is still light in the west. From my hotel window, the hammer and sickle that rise over the city square are silhouetted against a saffron sky. Last night we had our final service in Muhorŝibir. The believers here in this Siberian town are so isolated—few foreigners have ever been here before—that when Zhenna composed a farewell poem for us, she described me as "a man from Mars"! But the blessings here are their hunger for the Word and our fellowship in Christ that transcends language and borders. One lady, dear Galya, who is always smiling, wept over our farewell. The smile, thankfully, soon returned—for with Galya it can't stay away long. The last time I saw her, she was riding her bicycle back to her village four miles away. Until recently, she covered the distance on foot—and never missed a service, even in subzero weather.

We drove back to Ülan Üde this afternoon in the Udintsev's ancient van. Yesterday we were heading to a village to preach, and it broke down at the edge of town. After a night of triage, they assured us it would get us here. The gears crunched and the engine moaned—and once even quit—but it finally made it. I hope Vasily made it back home okay.

Despite all that, it was a beautiful afternoon. The summer sun is waking the land (and the mosquitos!) from a long sleep. Rich, dark earth is spattered with little, green shoots of wheat. Mongol cowboys drive their herds to shimmering streams, and we passed village after Buryat village where the gospel has yet to reach.

Spent the evening getting better acquainted with Ülan Üde. With four universities and a population of about four hundred thousand, this seems to be the best place to begin a work—and from here, reach out into the villages. A city official, a gentleman named Sergei, was very helpful. He is a friend of a friend of a friend, but he turned out to be a good contact. Like most Buryats, he is Buddhist, yet he seems curious about Christianity and promised to help us find a meeting place if Pavlo is able to organize a Ukrainian evangelistic team to come back here. Sergei took us on a nice walk of the city center, which ended at the main square, where sits a massive head of Lenin—thirty to forty feet high! It is a modern Ozymandias. How does that poem go?

Another Ozymandias

Half sunk, a shattered visage lies, whose frown,
And wrinkled lip, and sneer of cold command,
Tell that its sculptor well those passions read

Which yet survive, stamped on these lifeless things,
The hand that mocked them and the heart that fed:
And on the pedestal these words appear:
"My name is Ozymandias, King of Kings:
Look on my works, ye mighty, and despair!"
Nothing besides remains.
Round the decay of that colossal form boundless and bare
The lone and level sands stretch far away.[3]

Sands of change have swept over Lenin's evil empire. And here
in this distant corner of it, another kingdom is rising—one which
shall *never* end.

TASHKENT, UZBEKISTAN

Reached Tashkent this morning. A man named Asad met us late
tonight at the hotel where we are staying. We had never met before,
but we have a mutual friend in Tahir. As foreigners meeting with
Uzbek believers, Pavlo and I must be careful; so Asad is our quiet,
critical link. He drove us across the city to meet a wonderful Uzbek
Christian family. Amir and his wife Hadeel and their extended family shared supper with us. We all sat on the floor on bright tapestries
and pillows around a low table. Amir poured out steaming black tea
and then offered a prayer of thanks. As is the Uzbek custom here, we
prayed with open hands (a sign of our need to receive blessing and
help from the Lord). Then at the conclusion of the prayer, we raised
our hands to our heads and down over our faces (an acknowledg-
ment of the blessings that flow down from our heavenly Father).

Amir, the eldest son, was the first in his family to come to Christ.
That was in 1995, after several years of spiritual struggle. Because
Uzbek families are so tightly knit, with large, extended families
living together in a *mahalla* or community, an Uzbek Christian's
first persecutors are the most painful and personal—his own family. Amir's father, a man named Hasan, was furious. He cursed and
beat his son often. Amir's mother was ashamed of him; his brothers
and sisters scorned him.

And yet, because the family is close-knit, if the light of a transformed life shines there, despite every attempt to snuff it out, then it *will* crack the darkness and other family members *will* come to Christ! After a year, Amir's brother Timur came to the Lord, then his sister, then his brother-in-law, then several nieces and nephews. Another sister couldn't wait until spring to be baptized. With snow still on the ground (I saw the pictures), she and Amir waded into the icy river to give public testimony of her faith in Jesus Christ. Two years ago Amir baptized his mother, who is now no longer ashamed of her son or her Savior. Hasan, the man who cursed and beat his grown son with his fists, sat next to me at the table. Two months ago, he gave his heart to Jesus. As he told the story tonight with great joy, the passage in Galatians came to my mind. Speaking of the apostle Paul, it fits my new brother as well: "They only were hearing it said, 'He who used to persecute us is now preaching the faith he once tried to destroy.' And they glorified God because of me" (Gal. 1:23–24).

SAMARKAND, UZBEKISTAN

The Silk Road was not so smooth getting here, but the way is decked in spring. Fresh green fields are dotted with chocolate-colored sheep. Shepherdesses with leathery faces, their heads covered with bright chadors, lay beneath apricot trees now flecked with white buds that fall like snow in the spring breeze. At times the scenes make me think I'm in another century, when this was a major caravan route, part of the old Silk Road. Alexander the Great and Marco Polo crossed these plains, but I am abruptly returned to the present by a *militsia* checkpoint and the choking clouds of diesel fumes that follow lumbering transports vying for space with donkey carts.

Rain clouds gather over the Turkestan Range—the Tajik border—and darken the way to Samarkand. At a mountain pass along the way, we stopped by a roadside stand for lunch, which hung fresh from meat hooks—strips of this mutton were cut off and grilled *forshashlyk*. Put with large loaves of naan bread and a thick yogurt drink called kefir, it was a tasty meal. This was the kind of "restaurant" where there are no menus, and the bill is settled afterward with something just short of a fist fight.

Reached Samarkand, the city of kings and khans, in midafternoon. The old city is dominated by the Registan, with its turquoise-domed mosques and brightly-tiled madrassahs (Islamic schools) built centuries ago by Tamerlane, when he made Samarkand the capital of his great empire. The Registan mosques face three sides of a grand courtyard and are covered with a bright bric-a-brac of tiles set in ornate geometric patterns.

A couple of bucks secured the help of a guard in unlocking the iron gate to the minaret of the oldest mosque, Ulugbhek, which is one of the sacred sites of Islam. The climb up was steeply winding, dark, and narrow. From the top of this tower, the muezzins have for over five hundred years cried out the call to prayer, "There is one god, Allah, and Mohammed is his prophet." Today, though, from the top of this minaret, I proclaimed the truth instead. With a loud voice I said, "For there is one God, and there is one mediator between God and men, the man Christ Jesus, who gave himself as a ransom for all" (1 Tim. 2:5–6).

A cold wind swept the words out over the huddled rooftops below. I prayed that God would help us to be bold in proclaiming this message and not concede this land and its millions of souls to death.

As dusk settled over the city, we purchased several large, round loaves of naan, still hot from the *tandir* ovens. Dipping the warm bread into the honey we had earlier bought along the mountain road, we had our supper for the long, rainy drive back to Tashkent.

ON THE BORDER NEAR OSH

Spent the day with Lena and her team in the city. Theirs is the dangerous work of telling young people about Jesus. Ten years ago the Muslim government passed a law forbidding such evangelism. Yet Lena continues to reach hundreds of Muslim kids in Christian camps each summer. Camp is usually held for twelve days in widely scattered areas to the east. Each camp has about 120 young people, and 80 percent are Muslim.

Lena is the daughter and granddaughter of Christian prisoners. She knows what real fear, loneliness, loss, betrayal, hunger, and cold are. She knows what it's like to live in hiding—and to win souls. Her courage and her ministry have inspired a dedicated team to help her. Some of the boys and girls she led to the Lord years ago have now taken up the work with her.

"Underground" camp

Correspondence courses are one of the most effective tools of outreach in a Muslim country. Of course, the militant Islamists know that as well, and so Lena's post office boxes were confiscated years ago. Yet the Bible correspondence courses continue "underground." I met several from Lena's team who do this work—Tima, Sirah, Ruth, Zukra. They are the "sparrows" who quietly slip into neighborhoods, taking the Bread of Life to hungry children. It is a ministry that is conducted house-to-house and hand-to-hand, one that takes quiet courage—and for that they have a good teacher.

BAKU, AZERBAIJAN

Two days ago, reached Baku. Once Azerbaijan was considered a backwater borderland of the old Soviet Empire, but today it is oil-rich and strategically positioned between Russia and Iran.

I've found a little side street café called Ali & Nino's. It's an intimate space with plump couches covered in cordovan. Its smoky walls are decked with old photographs of men sporting fezzes, swords, and enormous mustaches. The only reminder here of what century I am actually in is a flat screen TV that has somehow elbowed its way in among the portraits and is blaring the latest Spiderman movie, dubbed in Russian.

It's a gray day in Baku. *Azerbaijan* is Persian for "land of fire," but today, a storm front is coming out of Iran, raking the city with cold winds and an occasional shower. Ali & Nino's offers a retreat, a cappuccino, and, from my table, a little window to the city and its people. Old babushkas, burrowed in fur from head to boot and looking so much like large muskrats, bend into the Caspian wind, as the younger set in the latest thing emerge from tony boutiques and brush past them.

Because the country is floating on oil and cash, Baku is a rich city—at least its rulers are. Everything here in the city center screams of conspicuous consumption—from the faux Versailles-style buildings to the poodle in a parka, squatting on the designer lawn nearby.

A ubiquitous sight here is the dictator Heydar Aliyev, portrayed on billboards, shop walls, and hotel lobbies—no words, just the old man wearing an awkward smile, as if he had little practice. There's something almost reptilian about it—like a snake that just swallowed something. Of course, Aliyev is grinning from the grave, because ten years ago he went to where all good dictators go. His son now looks after the "family business."

Azerbaijan is a post-Soviet police state—just one of many Stalinist spin-offs, complete with a dictator and a brutal secret police force. That, combined with a 99 percent Muslim population, makes the opportunities for gospel work bleak, and the percentages seem to add up to failure. All of that would be true if the Lord was sty-mied by statistics, but the gospel is "the power of God for salva-tion" (Rom. 1:16) and cannot be stopped.

At Ali and Nino's with Pavlo

This morning I met Pastor Huseyn, who shepherds a flock of over two hundred in Baku. We met in an abandoned dacha on the outskirts of the city, along a windswept stretch of the Caspian. Because of sophisticated surveillance technology, Huseyn and I dis-abled our cell phones and left them in another location. However, despite our precautions, Huseyn didn't look or sound hounded. In fact, Huseyn was jubilant, as if he knew something the govern-ment doesn't—the fact that Christ has already won! Despite con-stant pressure from the KGB—threats, fines, interrogations—the believers here are spreading the fame of Christ. Huseyn said that recently a law was passed raising the fine for passing out gospel tracts to three thousand dollars—about a year's wage. Not long ago some believers in his church were arrested for giving a tract to a man who asked for one—and then betrayed them. The po-lice officer asked the Christians why they were breaking the law.

They replied, "Because we are telling people about Jesus's love." The officer asked, "Did Jesus pass out tracts?" They looked at him puzzled. Then he said, "Just tell them about Jesus, but don't give out tracts." This gives "What Would Jesus Do" a whole new meaning. Huseyn laughed with delight in telling of our God's stunning, sovereign surprises—how he could turn a trip to the police station into a gospel strategy session!

These Christians are finding, making, and taking every opportunity to speak of Christ. One way was their outreach to the blind—people who in this society are shunned and helpless. These Azeri Christians found them, fed them, and taught them basic skills to care for themselves. And they told them about the One who loved the blind. So many of these blind Muslims came to Christ that the government has now prohibited this outreach—better to keep them blind in every sense of the word.

Since that door has closed, Huseyn's church is now reaching mentally disabled children who live in horrific state institutions. They are showing them love and sharing Christ with these young men and women. Now, whenever the pastor comes to visit, the kids shout, "Jesus is here!" Not only have many of these young people entered the kingdom as a little child, but several staff members have, too. They have no category for the kind of love that these Christians are showing week after week, month after month. Calvary love opened their eyes and hearts, and then Christ broke the chains of Islam off of them. Huseyn added, though, that they are already getting pressure to stop going to the asylums because the gospel is turning things upside down.

So here, on the edge of the old empire, history repeats itself. As the Muslims do just what the Communists did before them—make every effort to crush the church by expending their resources to prevent Christians from doing things like feeding the blind and loving kids with Down syndrome—these new tyrants should know better. Their failure is as certain as that of the old Soviet Empire. Christ is building his church here—and there is no stopping him.

2

CHILDREN OF CAIN

The Balkans

Mostar, Bosnia, during the siege

There is something dark about the Balkans. Sure, there are many places of light and beauty—I think of the picture-postcard scenes along Croatia's Dalmatian Coast, where red-tiled towns and amber shores meet the bottomless blue waters of the Adriatic. But the darkness I speak of is something deeper. It is dark—like charred rafters and bloodstains and widows' dresses.

Dame Rebecca West visited Yugoslavia in the 1930s and managed to squeeze six weeks of travel into some of the best eleven hundred pages of travel writing in the twentieth century. But the tragic history of the people is concisely captured in a single passage, in which she wrote:

> Were I to go down into the market-place, armed with the powers of witchcraft, and take a peasant by the shoulders and whisper to him, "In your lifetime, have you known peace?" wait for his answer, shake his shoulders and transform him into his father, and ask him the same question, and transform him in his turn to his father, I would never hear the word "Yes," if I carried my questioning of the dead back for a thousand years.[1]

In the wake of the Cold War, the Communists' grip on Yugoslavia loosened, and a country the size of Wyoming with three religions and twice that many major ethnic groups simply could not contain itself. Wars of nationalism and ethnic cleansing involving Serbs, Croats, Bosniaks, Albanians, Montenegrins, and Macedonians left more than one hundred thousand dead, displaced two million, and produced seven new countries. As it has often been said of the Balkans, "Too much history, too little geography."

Further south, Albania was shaking off five centuries of Ottoman rule, capped by a Communist era led by a brutal, bizarre tyrant named Enver Hoxha. Hoxha adored Stalin and successfully modeled his repressive regime after North Korea and crushed all religion. In 1992, when Communism fell, there was not a single church in the entire country. Ironically, the decade that followed was one of lawlessness, looting, wars on the northern border—and the rapid advance of the gospel!

Today gospel light is penetrating the darkness of the Balkans and transforming lives. The following journal entries trace the paths of two light-bearers: Pastor Miŝko in Croatia and Bosnia during the last year of the war and, more recently, David in Albania. David was one of the first to take the gospel into Albania, and he has discipled many over the years, multiplying the light of Christ's endless life and relentless grace on both sides of the northern border. Through these efforts, Christ is powerfully bringing men and women to himself in this bloodied region.

Should Dame West ask her question today: "In your lifetime have you known peace?" through the power of the gospel, there would be many here among the children of Cain who would answer, yes!

SOMEWHERE OVER THE ATLANTIC

The Virginia shore has long since slipped beyond the dark sea. Like an old man, these days the winter sun retires early, pulling a dusky blanket over his head as he beds down just beyond the horizon. My night flight takes me back to the Balkans, a land crushed beneath the boot print of war. For now, in the wake of a cease-fire, the Bosnian bloodletting has subsided. Whether this is peace or pause, only time will tell. Bosnia is a powder keg blanketed in snow right now, but great needs and, therefore, great opportunities are ahead. It is a weary hour, so enough for now.

DARUVAR, CROATIA

Miŝko met me at the snowy Zagreb airport. It's good to be with my dear friend again. Whenever I travel with this pastor and see how he stops and turns to—not away from—homeless, suffering refugees, whether Muslim, Croat, or Serb, I feel I'm on a bomb-cratered Jericho Road with the Good Samaritan.

Over supper we discussed Bosnian outreach—the urgency to get the gospel into Bosnia now, while there is less consolidation of Islam and greater openness among the war victims. One Croat missionary is already in Bosnia, in Novi Travnik, witnessing and gathering a little flock. If the snow and the Serbs permit, Miŝko and I will go to Novi Travnik in a few days. We must appeal to the Lord to send more courageous laborers into the Bosnian harvest—to Bihac, Banja Luka, Mostar, Gorazde, Zenica, Tuzla, Sarajevo—and to a million lost, shattered souls between. All of these unreached cities and more were on Miŝko's lips, as he prayed forcefully tonight.

Misˆko was raised in a poor, godless home here in northern Croatia. At the time, this was still part of Communist Yugoslavia, and the dictator Tito ruled with an iron fist. Misˆko grew up an atheist. Yet, as a teenager, he was shocked by the sudden death of his fourteen-year-old niece and haunted by the question, is there anything after death?

At the age of seventeen, looking for a better life in the West, Miŝko eluded the border guards and slipped into Italy. Being underage, he was held by the Italians in a refugee camp and later deported back to Yugoslavia, where he was promptly imprisoned. After his release, he was sent into the army and assigned to a kind of "Dirty Dozen" battalion made up mostly of ex-convicts.

Among his comrades was a man named Simo, who seemed to stand out from the rest. Miŝko and Simo soon struck up a friendship. Seven months passed before Miŝko understood why Simo was different—he was a Christian. Witnessing and having a Bible were criminal offenses, but one evening they talked quietly in a field about life and death. Simo told Miŝko the simple gospel story about how there was a God who loved him so much that he gave his Son to die for him and offered him eternal life. Miŝko immediately embraced the truth.

The change in this young soldier's life was dramatic. He took his entire month's wage to purchase a smuggled New Testament, and he read it through six times! He then borrowed a whole Bible and read it through. The Word was like water, cleansing sinful habits from his life. Miŝko also became bold in his witness to the other soldiers and to his family. Despite the fact that his father disowned him, his heavenly Father did not. Even in the face of persecution, God gave him boldness. Though there was opposition, there was also great hunger for the Word of God. Once a fellow soldier invited Miŝko to come to his village in Bosnia with the good news. It was winter, and heavy snowdrifts delayed his arrival. Miŝko hitchhiked as far as he could and then walked all night in waist-deep snow, reaching the town at four in the morning. Rather than finding the villagers asleep, they were still waiting up for him! By five o'clock, he had thawed out enough to preach, and the people of the town of Modrica received the Word with great gladness.

The years that followed have not dulled the kind of determination it took to push through the snow on that lonely, winter night long ago. Since Pastor Miŝko has been both a soldier and a refugee, it is an ironic providence that his church, during the first two years of the war, was thrust on the front line of fighting, and now he and his dear wife Mira continue to bind up the physical and spiritual wounds of the refugees. They have led Croats, Serbs, and Bosnian Muslims alike to the only peace that will last beyond this war.

It is nearly midnight, and too soon my alarm clock will call me out from beneath warm covers for a chilly meeting with the last day of the year.

DARUVAR, CROATIA

Arose early. After breakfast Miŝko and I drove about twenty miles out of Daruvar to the village of Korenicani. There we held Sunday services with some village folk who meet in the back room of an abandoned Orthodox church that is spattered from small arms fire. The little corner woodstove was the only source of heat on this frigid morning. Several walked a considerable distance through the snow to reach the church. Among the gathering were black-draped old women who were stooped and broken, weighed down from the hard labor of living. There were also some men and several young people—altogether more than a dozen in this little flock. Three years ago the war swept through this village. After the dead were buried, the refugees fled, and the young were called to arms, only two Christians remained in this church. So though the numbers are small, the growth is encouraging—a sign of life in this battle-scarred village.

I was asked to preach, and Miŝko interpreted. My text was Mark 5:24–34. The woman, who seized her single opportunity to get to the Savior, is a picture of all of us—poor, needy, and dying. Because of the intense cold, Miŝko and I both kept our heavy coats on in the pulpit, our words punctuated with frosty breath.

Afterward, Miŝko and I visited Hajrudin, his wife Behija, and their daughters. This Bosnian Muslim family lost everything in the war and were forced to flee to Croatia. They ended up in a refugee camp near Daruvar, and through the compassionate help of Miŝko and the church, they opened their hearts to the gospel.

Behija was pleased to learn that we will attempt to reach Sarajevo when we travel to Bosnia in a few days. She has two brothers there—Ibrahim and Muradif—whom she has not seen since the war began. It will be great if somehow we can see these two Muslim men and give them some supplies, family news, and the gospel!

Over thick Turkish coffee, we talked until well into the night. While they have found new life here, they are also trying to figure out how to pick up the pieces of the life that has been forever crushed by war. Add to that, Hajrudin and Behija are under considerable strain these days over the care of Hajrudin's sick mother. The old woman lay quite still under some ragged quilts in a corner cot and appears to be near death.

NOVI TRAVNIK, BOSNIA

Set out for Bosnia this morning. It is now nearing midnight, with the occasional sound of heavy weapons firing to provide assurance that I am really here. I will try to record something of this day of providences as Miŝko and I set out from Croatia.

From funds Christians provided in the States, we brought just over five thousand dollars with us for refugee ministry. In addition, I purchased several kilos of coffee in small packages for gifts. This is a treasured commodity here! We drove through a light snow to Zagreb and then to Karlovac but found the more direct road to central Bosnia too dangerous to take. Instead, we were forced to make a ten-hour trek, traveling roughly southward to Knin, then looping northward through central Bosnia.

The road from Karlovac to Knin is heavily marked by war. This was the Serbian-occupied region, where fierce and strategic fighting took place this past August when the Croatian Army liberated the territory. Some signs of recovery appear—the bombed-out bridge over the Korana River has fortunately been repaired, and we were able to cross without delay. In Slunj, a single strand of Christmas lights across the cratered main road gave the place a flicker of life. With the minefields cleared at Plitvice, the resort was open; so, we warmed ourselves with good cappuccinos before continuing on the icy road. Further south, though, the destruction was complete. At Gracac, the only sign of life was the digging of fresh graves for newly discovered corpses. Here and there along the road, discarded ammunition boxes were strewn in the haste of battle, and bullet-riddled cars still litter the roadside.

Misko on the road to Novi Travnik, Bosnia

Got a quick supper and kept moving, conscious of the descending night. Drove to Novi Travnik by way of Bugogno along a treacherous, ice-packed, bomb-cratered road. The mountain pass was even more complicated because of a NATO convoy of tanks and minesweepers stalled by a jack-knifed transport. Reached our destination late and checked into the "Hotel Novi Travnik"—what luxury! The elevator is broken, and one wing destroyed by artillery fire. But it's really OK—I have clean sheets and running water and electricity, which is better than what many have in this ravaged land.

After checking in, we visited a refugee family in Novi Travnik. Radovan and his wife Blazenka are some of the first fruits of the gospel here. Blazenka, whose name means "grace," received Christ after hearing the testimony of a Bosnian refugee who had been saved after fleeing to Switzerland. When this woman returned to her village, she witnessed to her neighbors, and Blazenka heard the gospel and believed. Blazenka then hastened home to tell her family what Jesus had done. Radovan heard his wife's testimony and immediately responded that he, too, wanted to be saved. The Lord had been preparing Radovan for two years for this moment. This is what Radovan told me tonight: When the war first swept through this region, he and his family were forced to flee their home to another part of the city, where they hunkered down in an abandoned apartment. One of the few things left there was a Bible—a book that, as a Communist, Radovan had always despised. However, because of snipers, the only time that he could leave the apartment for food or firewood was at night—he had long days with little to do but read. So Radovan picked up the Bible and read—he read it through three times! The Lord was plowing up the hard heart of a disillusioned atheist, preparing it for the good seed of Blazenka's gospel witness. Radovan has now taken up that Bible he found and is sharing Christ, bringing light to this very dark place.

It is late now, and with occasional shots ringing out, maybe I should turn out the lights in my room before someone does it for me! Whether we will reach Sarajevo tomorrow is unclear, but we set out at first light.

SARAJEVO, BOSNIA

My journey to Sarajevo began this morning with a man from Kathmandu. We found the NATO outpost somewhere near Travnik, where we asked a Nepalese soldier attached to the British NATO command here about the road from Kiseljak. He gave us the all-clear, and so we went on. There was some problem on the road with Serbs slowing traffic, but a detachment of the French Legion cleared the way, and we continued on to Kiseljak, where a swarm of Karadzic's troops milled about the road. We were then within Serbian lines.

Entering Sarajevo was like driving down a corridor of hell. The towering apartment buildings are now high-rise horrors—blackened, blasted hulks, some even teetering on collapse. The ample avenue that enters the city from the west is a wasteland. Battle-scarred, abandoned, bullet-riddled streetcars are lined up waiting for no one. Here and there in the median of the avenue, pathetic little garden patches, hastily planted during the siege, lay wilted beneath the winter mud. Sniper Alley was quiet this afternoon, but just this morning a NATO soldier was shot here by a sniper—another easy, anonymous killing.

Stopped briefly at the Sarajevo Holiday Inn and the defiant office tower of the newspaper *Oslobodenje*. Here the killing began four sad years ago, when snipers fired on a peace demonstration. This became the flashpoint for Bosnia's war, the first draw of blood that since has claimed tens of thousands of dead and wounded.

Continued on to the city center, near the mortar-pocked square where the Marketplace Massacre occurred. We stopped for supper at the Ragusa Taverna, a dark inviting café surrounded with a parapet of sandbags. This gave us a base from which to place calls and have meetings. While at the Ragusa, I befriended a little boy named Mirza, and through him got acquainted with his parents. Mirza, whose name means "for peace," was born ten days before the war began. He has known nothing but the siege, despite his hopeful name. His parents were very warm and even helped us contact Behija's brothers. Before leaving, I gave this Muslim family a "Jesus" tract.

While waiting for Behija's brothers, Ibrahim and Muradif, to reach the Ragusa, Miŝko and I took a walk in the waning light. Flurries fell as we walked the narrow cobblestone street of Sarajevo's old Baŝcarŝija district, where I purchased a little silver *ibrik* for Debbie. Power was restored ten days ago, so there was light—and hope—in the air. One shopkeeper, upon learning I was an American, gave me a gift of a little brass plate etched with the name "Sarajevo." She said she gave it to me because America had done so much for her city and for peace.

Along the way, I found the Sarajevo street corner where on June 28, 1914, a Bosnian Serb assassinated Austrian Archduke Franz Ferdinand. This murder along the muddy Miljacka River in an obscure corner of Europe ignited the twentieth century's First World War—sending the Great Powers to the trenches of France and Flanders, and millions, like the prince, to an untimely grave.

I noticed that this fateful avenue was pocked with craters from mortar grenades rained on Sarajevo during *this* war. On that spot I picked up a piece of shrapnel—a hard, sharp reminder that "the war to end all wars" ended nothing.

Walked back to the Ragusa in time to meet Ibrahim and Muradif. Over supper we heard their siege stories, passed along family news and a photograph from Behija, and Miŝko shared the good news with them. It's late, but we can't stay in Sarajevo. We'll catch the coattail of some NATO convoy and head back to Novi Travnik tonight.

ON THE ROAD SOMEWHERE IN WESTERN BOSNIA

Miŝko and I slipped out of Sarajevo last night under a cloak of darkness, thankfully without incident. Yet a strange sense of frustration hangs over me, especially knowing that soon I'll be on a plane, headed back home, leaving Miŝko and Mira, Radovan, Blazenka, and others to minister among the ruins and ruined. I must return.

Because of a rockslide near Gornji Vakuf, we took a narrow, ice-packed, mountain passage called the Emerald Road. It turned out to be a treacherous trek—a twisted ribbon of ice on which vehicles, including those of a British NATO convoy failing to reach the summit, slid backward. But by God's grace, we cleared the Komar Range.

We are in western Bosnia now. My seemingly tireless friend is showing the strain, and fuel is a concern—perhaps another hour to the Croatian border. But our sense of isolation—of the enormity of the desolation—settles over us with sickening silence. This land is as lifeless as a moonscape. Lusnic, Sakovic, Crni Lug, Bosansko Grahovo—every village, every town, every home, in every direction—destroyed. Like open sepulchers, the roofless dwellings shelter their dead. The wind in this valley, which has long since carried away the shrieks of the murdered, now plays among the abandoned tanks, discarded ammunition boxes, and charred walls. Otherwise, it is quiet—absolute, terrible silence.

TIRANA, ALBANIA

Arrived in Tirana about noon. David and Kristi were there to welcome me. David is a dear friend and brother, a frontline soldier in the kingdom's advance in Albania. We have shared much together since his earliest days here.

After storing my gear, I took a walk to the old square in the heart of the capital. The impressive statue of Skanderbeg keeps watch over the bustling center. The heroic Skanderbeg defended Albania against the Turks, stalling the advance of Islam during his lifetime. Ironically, his equestrian figure sits in the shadow of a mosque, for Islam now claims much of the country. Nearby are the remnants of Albania's disastrous years of Communism. Facing the square is a huge mosaic of men and women from every corner of the country. Their adoring faces look down upon—or rather *used* to look down upon—a giant bronze image of the dictator Enver Hoxha. Hoxha brought a brand of Communism and cult worship that would have been the envy of Stalin or Mao. He declared the religion of Albania to be atheism—but Hoxha was a cheap cheat who cleared the deck of all other gods so that he alone would be worshipped. School children even wrote love letters to him addressing Hoxha as their "daddy." He destroyed the mosques and churches, burned the Bibles and every scrap of religious literature. He cut Albania off from the outside world, and in a kind of national psychosis, he convinced his people they were under threat of imminent attack from America. He told them that their poverty was wealth and their hope was Hoxha. It was one of the longest and most successful lies in history.

After Hoxha's death, Albania slowly shook off its shackles. It was the last of the Iron Curtain dominoes to fall after the Berlin Wall came down. Pulling down Hoxha's statue was the grand finale. The white marble pedestal where it stood is now cracked, littered, and smells like a latrine. The people have moved on, pursuing other gods of their own making.

Returned to David and Kristi's home and had a quiet evening with the family after a long day.

SHKODRA, ALBANIA

Up early. I awoke to hungry breakfast smells—the aroma of cinnamon rolls, eggs, and good coffee. Kristi was already busy in the kitchen, getting breakfast ready. She would make Martha Stewart jealous. Her table is always one of grace and good taste. Kristi is a pretty, petite lady, but inside she's rock solid. I recall once during the time of anarchy that Kristi was feeding her little girl Sophie when shooting started in the street below their window. She calmly moved the highchair away from the window, and continued spooning in the rice cereal without missing a beat!

After breakfast we headed north to Shkodra, stopping briefly to stock up on supplies for our long journey into the mountains—a trail mix of sardines, Snickers, and cans of cold coffee. Reached Shkodra about noon, and met Beni and his wife Linda. Pastor Beni was the firstfruit of David's work in Shkodra, when he came here sixteen years ago. David had been here for only six weeks when he met Beni, who was then a junior in high school. Of course, David wasn't much older when he came to Albania—just twenty-one, just out of college, just over from America. David led Beni to Christ and then went deep into the mountains to his village to share Christ with the rest of Beni's family. Beni now holds a doctorate in American literature from a university in Austria. He is a tentmaker—teaching at the University of Shkodra and pastoring the church that David planted here. Beni's leadership, humility, and joy attract the lost to Christ and also reflect David's mentoring.

Went on to Rozafa Castle—one of my favorite places. It's a strategic, stubborn citadel that keeps watch over Shkodra. Invaders could not ignore it—nor easily take it. Over the centuries, thousands tried and failed to conquer what was called "the eagle's nest." It usually finally fell only through hunger or treachery. From its battlements, we had a magnificent view of the rivers that breach the mountains to the east and north and of Lake Scutari, which lay in silver light. David and I talked of fishing—and of fishing for men. This is his Mount of Olives, his place to pray over the city.

David, gospel pioneer

SHKODRA, ALBANIA

David and I met up with Theresa this morning. For years she has reached the women of the mountains—the women that are hard to get to. These women are often regarded as no more than beasts of burden—good mostly for carrying things like babies, water, and firewood. Theresa has loved many of them into Christ's kingdom.

On the drive, Theresa told me how the Lord led her to leave America and serve him here in Albania. Really remarkable, because in part, it began on the worst day of Theresa's life—it was the morning she learned her husband was divorcing her. Her heart was shattered beneath the weight of the pain. Later that morning, Theresa was driving to the school where she was a teacher. Naturally, she was crying and thought, "I'll be at school soon. I have to compose myself." She pulled up to a stoplight, and looking down, she saw a long-stemmed rose wrapped in paper lying next to her car. Since the light was still red, she got out and picked it up. The red petals were perfect, fresh, and fragrant. The light was still red; so she looked it over. There was no name of the giver or recipient—not even the florist—on it; but tucked down in the paper was a little typed note, which said simply, "I love you, you are special." Theresa took the rose as from the Lord's hand and thought, "He is saying to me, as it were, I will be your husband. I will give you roses for the rest of your life." From there, the Lord would lead her step by step to Albania, where she has served for a dozen years now, ministering to orphans and working among poor, trodden-down village women—everywhere spreading the fragrance of Christ and a passion for her Beloved. The rose has its thorns, but Jesus said, "Whoever loses his life for my sake will find it" (Matt. 10:39). And here, with joy, Theresa has found her life in the rugged borderlands of High Albania.

Theresa, David, and I went to Laç to visit Mark and his daughter Dava. Mark was recently bedridden from a terrible accident, in which he was knocked from a high ladder by the force of an electric shock. This was the first time after his fall that Theresa had seen the man she affectionately calls "Baç"—"Daddy." It wasn't always this way. In fact, Mark once threatened to kill Theresa because Mark's youngest daughter, Prenda, had become a Christian. David had led her to the Lord, and Kristi and Theresa had discipled her. Mark was furious. He beat his daughter—and even told her he would rather she were a prostitute than a Christian. Dava was equally hateful to her sister, taking Prenda's Bible and tearing it apart. Dava told me, "For some people, coming to Christ is a war—for me it was a war." With laughter she added, "Theresa was 'fishing,' but when she caught me, she hooked a shark!" Dava said this as if she were talking about another person, which she was!

In the war for her soul, Dava surrendered and became a radically different person—like being born a second time. Her son, Ervis, believed too, and it was actually Ervis's calm but persuasive witness that finally led his grandfather to Christ. It was winter, and the woodstove was making the room dark and smoky. Ervis said to his grandpa, "Your life is like this room. Why don't you open your life to the light and the fresh air of Christ?" Mark, broken by the weight of his sin, flung open the window of his heart and received Jesus. The clouds lifted, darkness became light, and hate was changed to love. The man who once threatened to kill Theresa now loves her like a daughter, and Dava loves her like a sister, which she is! The Bible-ripper now embraces the Christian magazines that Theresa brought for her. In that little room was the glow of the gospel; their stunning faces were brightened by joy because they have met Jesus. Between them and with their Savior are bonds of forgiveness deeper than blood, stronger than death.

Went on to visit Dila, another sister of Prenda's. We were warmly received in Dila's village. Theresa's love has opened the hearts of so many here. While helping them plant a garden, she adds seeds of her own from Scripture. Sitting with them while they tend sheep, she tells them how "all we like sheep have gone astray" (Isa. 53:6) and how the Good Shepherd brings us to himself.

Many gathered and greeted us with singing and playing of a two-stringed, long-necked, lute-like instrument called a *ciftili*, and there were grapes and figs and laughter and sharing in the Word together. Theresa told me afterward that one of the girls said to her, "You have come to visit me! I am so happy I feel I could fly!" Theresa has won their hearts, and they have won hers, too. Far from the headlines, though very much on the front lines, Theresa's simple gifts of time and acts of love have brought the kingdom of Christ to another mountain village.

One more visit before nightfall. Near Rubik, we crossed the Fan River by footbridge. Theresa took some clothes and school supplies for the children of a sister in Christ named Dalina. Her husband Nikoll still needs the Lord. David took the opportunity on this visit to speak clearly and directly to Nikoll of his need. While David was in one room witnessing to Nikoll, Theresa, Dalina, and the kids were in another room. The children sang gospel songs, but they were also praying for their daddy that he would receive Jesus.[2]

BAJRAM CURRI, ALBANIA

David and I bedded down for another night on the kitchen floor, but sleep is difficult tonight. It seems that on certain nights—this being one of them—it is open season on stray dogs, and a small bounty is paid for them. Out in the street, the gunfire, drunken laughter, loud curses, and cries of wounded dogs all combined to make sleep difficult—so I will try to catch up on my writing instead.

Yesterday, we took the ferry to Tropoja, which chugs up a flooded gorge, turning a stomach-churning, cliff-hanging, all-day road trip into a two-hour tour of Albania's magnificent mountains. We docked at Fierze and drove on to Bajram Curri, the main city of the rugged Tropoja region that borders Kosovo. Bajram Curri is a hard place, where Islam and guns rule. An al-Qaeda cell here has added to the violence and to the hatred of the cross.

We're staying at the home of Astrit and Vjollca. Astrit pastors the little group of believers that dot this region like candles. I love this faithful couple—I love to see *their* love. In Albanian culture, a man can beat or rape his wife, and it's considered normal. Men sometimes even get their wives by kidnapping them—and usually their relationship goes downhill from there. But Astrit is a Christian husband, and Vjollca is a Christian wife; and so their marriage is a new creation in Christ, too. Astrit is also a Christian father, so he loves his daughters as he loves his son. In the culture here, girls are generally unwelcomed and unwanted, but the gospel is transforming that kind of thinking every day in this home. Vjollca is a special lady who has endured the death of a son and threats upon their lives. Yet their doors and cupboards are always open to strangers and poor children. Vjollca's name means "purple flower," like those growing by her doorstep. The perfume of her life is broken and poured out to the Lord, and its fragrance fills a city that has only known the stench of death.

Today is the Lord's Day. Went early to a nearby town to meet with believers in a little room of an apartment overlooking the Valbona River. This church was born out of a simple three-step process, as David puts it in uncomplicated actions items: Pray. Meet people. Tell them about Jesus. For four years he prayed as he made trips by ferry up the river. The first believer here was a young woman named Migena. She has never lost her first love. After she believed, Migena immediately, spontaneously told people about Jesus, and they believed. She first led her brother to Christ, and then others came, too. They met by the riverbank. They had two Bibles and no hymnbooks, but that didn't matter to them—they were so glad to have Jesus! Migena taught them the songs she had memorized in Shkodra, and they took turns reading the Bible and sharing the joy they were discovering.

Joy is still the hallmark of this simple church. Astrit led the service this morning, and I preached from Isaiah 53 of Christ, our Passover, who took our sins upon himself that we might live. Afterward, three were baptized in the cold Valbona. They shared the river with cows wading in for a drink. We had to keep a low profile, for there are much opposition and hateful, malicious, ridiculous rumors about these Christians. Rumors like: "They baptize naked." "Their worship is an orgy." "They poison children." Interesting that these are the same vicious lies that circulated among the Romans against Christians in the first century. Why is it the Devil doesn't need a new lexicon of lies after twenty centuries? Because the old ones still work. David says, though, that the best way to fight lies is with truth. The liars then have to modify their lies in order to remain credible. And so light scatters darkness, and joy shatters fear. I saw it in their faces today.

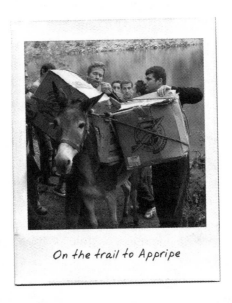

On the trail to Appripe

BAJRAM CURRI, ALBANIA

It is late as I take up my pen. My usual dilemma—I need to sleep, and I need to write. I'll write. I awoke this morning at five o'clock to the sound of a rushing, mighty rain. My heart sank for it seemed our plans to go up into the mountains were washing away like the torrents that beat on the roof. I lay in bed and prayed for an hour that the Lord would fulfill his purposes for the day, and that I would trust him with the answer. He gave me peace.

Although our original plans had to be canceled, the sky began to break in the east, and even though drizzle fell, Astrit decided we could still make it to a village that had yet to hear the gospel. After breakfast we loaded up some Christmas boxes that had been left over from the distribution earlier this year and set out for Appripe, a village scattered over the face of one of the mountains along the river. As we drove, Astrit greeted truck drivers and truant schoolboys out fishing, and he gave a hitchhiker a ride. Astrit is soul-conscious, always reaching out to people. These are his mountains, the place where he was born; and these are his people, the ones he has been sent to tell good news.

The way was rugged but beautiful. At one point along the crest of the road, the river was a perfect mirror. It was as if the world were upside down—with the sky below us and the clouds like icebergs floating in liquid jade. A boat's bow cut through this canvas and broke my reverie.

We took the Land Rover as far as she could go and then hauled the boxes down to the river, where boys from the village had already brought a boat over to meet us. On the farther shore, we loaded a donkey with the Christmas boxes. The path was steep, and we had a good climb. I thought of the verse in Isaiah, "How beautiful upon the mountains are the feet of him who brings good news" (Isa. 52:7). I think that applies whether it's two feet or four hooves! The switchback trail led us to a schoolhouse and some scattered dwellings. The donkey was rewarded with a little grass, and he seemed happy enough. I was happy, too, for this was the first time the gospel has gone to this village. Forty-five children plus teachers were packed into the little schoolhouse. Astrit shared Christ with them all and encouraged the students to work hard at their studies. We gave the gifts to all the children, and Astrit gave New Testaments to the teachers. Outside, David witnessed to shepherds. With all the bright packages, shepherds, students, and their wisemen hearing the "good news of great joy that will be for all the people" (Luke 2:10)—and even a donkey, thrown in for good measure—it seemed I had a little glimpse of Bethlehem. Despite what the calendar says, this was their first real Christmas. But I think of all the other unreached villages, pocketed deep within the Tropojan range—places that have never had a day like this, never heard the gospel—there it's another Narnia, where it's "always winter and never Christmas."[3]

On the way back we turned off the road and went to Arvej and to the remnants of the house where Astrit grew up. It's now abandoned and ruined. It was an emotional time for David and Astrit. More than just the house, this was the place where David hiked to many years ago, and this is where he led Astrit to the Lord. These are the fields where David discipled a shepherd boy who, like him, became a gospel pioneer and pastor. And this is where we prayed and praised the One who called us and gave us such a beautiful day of ministry.

Tonight we plotted the way we will take in the morning. The war in Kosovo gave missionaries in Albania opportunities for a bold advance to reach Albanians there. A new road cuts from here through the mountains into Kosovo—and from there into Montenegro—giving access to some of the least-reached parts of what was Yugoslavia. That's the road we will take.

PEJË, KOSOVO

Crossed the border into Kosovo without incident. Two things stood out as we entered Kosovo—signs of life and signs of death. It is the first week of school, and so giggly girls with pink, sparkly Barbie backpacks were walking to school—walking past cemeteries of the war dead and monuments of the mass murders that took place in town after town. It's the wake of war that Serbia unleashed against the Albanians in Kosovo in a campaign of ethnic cleansing. Eventually NATO bombs and troops quelled the killing, but not before ten thousand were dead and a million more were displaced.

Stopped in Dečani to pay respects at one of the memorials. All the men and teenage boys here were gathered and murdered on a single day, April 1, 1999, by Serbian soldiers—well, more like serial killers in uniforms.

Went on to Pejë, which the Serbs call Peć. During the war, nearly every home here was destroyed, and there are still a few remnants of the bombings, but for the most part the red tile roofs mark the rebuilding—a city coming back to life—but now under Albanian control and NATO protection.

Here, David introduced me to his friends, missionaries Keith
and Pam. After a quick coffee, Keith took us up to the Christian
camp they are building high in the mountains. The rugged road
to the camp begins with a NATO checkpoint bristling with razor
wire, followed by rockslides, occasional landmine markers, hairpin
curves, and a couple of narrow log bridges over rapids the color
of turquoise ice. The camp is set among snowcapped peaks and is
slowly taking shape through the vision and just plain hard work of
Keith and Pam.

Keith and Pam's preparation for missionary service wasn't done
in a seminary, but rather on a farm in Iowa, where they raised corn
and five kids. But farming turned out to be preparation for another
kind of plowing and sowing and reaping. They came to Albania a
dozen years ago, in the middle of life, first making short-term trips
and then, like the parable of treasure in a field, with joy they sold
all to follow Christ here. Soon after arriving in Shkodra, the war in
Kosovo sent thousands of Kosovar Albanians streaming into their
city. Keith and Pam went to the widows and orphans in their need,
loved them, wept with them, and told them about Jesus. When the
killings and bombings stopped, they returned to Kosovo with them
and helped rebuild their homes. They are still here visiting the widows and fatherless in their affliction (James 1:27). This will be the
third summer they have hosted Kosovar kids at this mountainside
camp. Some are orphans of the war dead; many are poor children
from the villages; most are Muslims—and all hear the gospel and
see it lived out. Keith and Pam give me hope in this land of untimely
graves. Their love in action is transforming a mountainside and
drawing children to Jesus—a generation that has known only war
and fear.

Returned to Pejë at last light in search of supper and a bed.

EARLY MORNING, PEJË, KOSOVO

A pesky rooster, in league with a Muslim belting out the first
call to prayer of the day, all conspired to wake me early. That's

when I found there was no electricity. I can't sleep anyway, and I can't forget a widow named Floria, who I met yesterday. I had asked Keith if I could see some of the houses he had rebuilt after the war and visit with the families. And so we drove out toward the Serbian border near the town of Izbic´—a sleepy, picturesque place now forever stained by the massacre that occurred there. That's where I met Floria. She and her daughter Rezmia were home. We brought them some groceries and left some money, and we talked and prayed; but for me it was a time to mourn with those who mourn.

I asked to see a photograph of Floria's husband. His name was Hamdi Tamaj, and I learned we were the same age. He and Floria had six children. When the Serbs came, they pulled his daughter from his arms and took him away with the other men of Izbic´. Half the men and boys they gunned down, and the other half they burned alive packed in the village schoolhouse. Altogether in a single day, every man in the village was killed—one hundred and forty of them. On that one day, March 28, 1999, Floria lost her husband, her father, her three brothers, and her husband's brother. Floria then fled fifty miles to Albania on foot with her six children—and gave birth to her seventh along the way of her trail of tears.

We went on to walk through the killing fields of Izbić. Wooden stakes in the Muslim fashion marked the graves. Rotted wreaths added their decay to this hopeless, senseless place. Here are fathers and sons and brothers, buried as they died—side by side, a torrent of souls rushed into eternity. I felt the sting of death there—I still feel it. There was no cross raised on that hillside, no reminders of grace. Their blood cries out from the ground, and I have no answer for them except unspeakable sadness over this tearing of life. This place is haunted by silence—or perhaps I am haunted by my own.

The killing fields of Izbic, Kosovo

BUDVA, MONTENEGRO

Cold rain was falling in Pejë as we set out for Montenegro. Stopped at a *pastiqerie* on the edge of town for a quick breakfast. We intended to grab and go, but the alluring pastries and the aroma of coffee persuaded us to savor the moment! Afterward, we started our ascent to the border. The roads were slick as we swung around switchbacks, and the engine groaned and struggled as we made our crab-like climb to the summit to the border crossing. Landmine markers were reminders to keep on moving.

Montenegro means "black mountain," but "black" was also the name given by its invaders—Turks and Venetians whose armies were swallowed up by the impregnable ranges. Black was the darkness of death and despair, for here men lost their courage, their way, and their lives in these tangled mountains. Our road took us through a range called *Prokletije*, which means the "accursed mountains" or "mountains of the damned." It's an old name, it's an old curse, and yet it's ironic that these mountains wall up a people that are among the least reached with the gospel in all of Eastern Europe. And so our prayer was that we find these people, particularly ethnic Albanians in Montenegro, having heard of enclaves of Albanians living deep within the mountains about Gusinje.

Last night we prayed that the Lord would direct our very steps today. David and I were in these mountains last year, but we found no Albanians and only a closed door. So we are continuing to knock. If we find ethnic Albanians in Montenegro, believers in Albania can make cross-border contact and share the gospel with them. There's a new road being cut from here to Tropoja, and David anticipates that in time, border crossings will ease up for Albanians. But at least for today we were warned we could be shot if we took the new road—so maybe next time.

The "accursed mountains" form a high wall around people who have yet to hear the good news, but the walls are coming down! I thought of the verse in Isaiah where it says, "I will make all my mountains a road" (Isa. 49:11). As we drove along, a little Albanian flag on a grave caught David's eye—a sure sign of Albanians! So David pulled off the road near a school and planned to talk to the teacher. As we crossed the road, a lady was walking a boy home from school. David greeted her in Albanian, and she greeted him back in Albanian!

Her name was Fatima, and she invited us to her brother's home, where she lives. So a door was opened to us! There we met Feris and Drita and their children. They offered us wonderful hospitality, wild blueberry compote, and cups of chestnut honey, which we washed down with Turkish coffee that was just as thick and sweet. While we got acquainted and savored such sweet providence, Fatima sat taking long drags on one cigarette after another—and hanging on our every word.

I noticed a covered cradle—in it Feris and Drita's daughter was sleeping. She looked like an angel, auburn ringlets framed her face, which was as clear and fair as porcelain. She was swaddled, bound from her shoulders to her feet with strips of cloth. It was interesting to see this old custom still practiced here and then to see her mother loose her and set her free! Her name is Era, which means "wind" and, with the help of some M&M's, we became friends.

Amazingly, we learned Drita's sister went to school with Pastor Beni's aunt. This is significant, for here ties of family and clan are stronger than lines on a map. David spoke to them, not of religion but of being born-again. Hearing this was a first for them, but the door is open to more gospel conversations. David and Feris exchanged phone numbers and promises to see each other again.

I think of David's simple formula for planting churches: pray, meet people, tell them about Jesus. Last night we prayed over this day. We gave God a day that was unarranged, and he took it and designed it as only he could. With grace and, I think, his wonderful sense of humor, God used a chain-smoking, Muslim woman named Fatima to open a closed door. The Lord worked on both sides of that door, ordering our steps and seconds to bring us to this beginning.

As we began our journey back to Albania, we drove along the canyon that walls the Morača River with soaring stone. David and I came across an old, rotting footbridge that spanned the river. Even though we had miles to go before we sleep, we couldn't resist exploring it and enjoying the growing expanse of land and sky.

We followed the river path to the sea, and the road led us out to where the mountains plunge into the Adriatic. Its colors exhaust my vocabulary to name every hue of blue. The sea breeze felt like freedom, and my heart is as light as the hawks that wheeled in the wind. We have seen Christ write another page of his acts today. The first open door to a family deep within the Black Mountains was a beginning—perhaps a small one, but like a clear mountain spring that falls and flows, gathering force until it joins the sea; so Lord Jesus, gather these also into your great kingdom!

SHKODRA, ALBANIA

We were out early this morning. Today brings the Muslim fasting month of Ramadan to a close, and so the streets were bustling in preparation for the celebration of *Eid*. David had a few errands to run, and so we walked and talked and invited people to church tomorrow.

Afterward we visited Fredi and Prenda. I was able to tell Prenda about our visit with her dad and with her sister Dava last week. Prenda is a trophy of grace, and her joy is contagious. Persecution never silenced her witness nor diminished her love. Her decision to follow Christ as a twenty-year-old college student has directly or indirectly resulted in over forty of her family members also trusting Christ—the gospel is viral! She and her husband, Fredi, minister to orphans in the city and to the poor, scorned gypsies on the outskirts of it.

Fredi and Prenda also demonstrate a counterculture view of family—one that reflects transformed thinking. Daughters, especially if they are the firstborn, are a mark of bad luck in many Albanian homes. The father curses, and the mother weeps, knowing the hardships the girl will face. Fredi and Prenda's first child was a girl. Rather than cursing, they blessed her with the name Edona, which means, "she is loved."

Early evening—an imam's long sermon, marking the end of Ramadan, mingled with the city sounds in the darkening streets. David, Fredi, and I drove out to a settlement of Shiite gypsies. The gypsies are outcasts, and so are their dwellings. Their tents and shacks are set along the Buna River amid a dump that is bordered by an open sewer. The door to this dump was opened with warm greetings to David and Fredi, familiar friends here. Their place is called "Chadrat," which simply means, "the tents." Recently, ten families were burned out of their homes here, and so the Christians in the Shkodra church gave wood to them to rebuild their homes. Our visit was the first time to see the finished work.

We were welcomed to their world because Fredi and David and their families have spent countless days with them. They have embraced them, taught their children, sang their songs, danced their dances, grieved over their graves, and told them about the Savior.

These people are scorned, hated, and dismissed as dirty beggars and thieves. Actually, that's what some of them are, but dirt never stopped Calvary love!

"He has made me glad."

The gypsy children quickly adopted us. They are ragged, beautiful children with eyes that dance while they sing, and we had a good time singing. Sidi, a brother, played guitar for us. He, too, comes here often—he has a heart for these poor ones. We sang *"ai me ngazelloi, ai me ngazelloi."* "He has made me glad, he has made me glad. I will rejoice, for he has made me glad." And our joy was added to tonight when one of the gypsy men, Ghazi, who David has patiently and repeatedly explained the gospel to, said he wanted to publicly identify with Christ!

The first stars rise above the old castle, and I can say over this day and over all the days here, "He has made me glad!"

3
TEN SPARROWS

China

The Temple of Heaven

Ironically—no, more like providentially—China's rise on the world stage coincides with its rise as a gospel force. The number of Chinese Christians may now be approaching one hundred million, and a truly Chinese church movement is underway, reaching the teeming coastal cities, spreading like wildfire across the central grasslands, and pushing westward to the walls of the Himalayas and beyond.

From the starting point of the modern missions movement two hundred years ago, China's size (the largest) and distance (the farthest) was magnetic—at least for men and women with a big enough view of the gospel to go. China was to missionaries what Everest was to mountain climbers. Before reaching Guangzhou in 1807, pioneer missionary Robert Morrison struggled between taking the gospel to China or Timbuktu and prayed "that God would station him in that part of the missionary field where the difficulties were greatest and to all human appearances, the most insurmountable."[1] Morrison chose China. Around the same time, William Carey wrote, "To know the will of God, we need an open Bible and an open map."[2] There was a reckless abandon about Christians who started at the back pages of an atlas to find God's will—but then, cross-bearing Christ-followers are all about reckless abandon.

To get a fuller picture of the gospel's story in China, I stopped in England to retrace a place of beginnings—of reckless abandon at the edge of the sea.

BRIGHTON BEACH, ENGLAND

Arrived at Heathrow yesterday and was met by my friend Roger. We have been transatlantic pen pals for years, so it was fun to finally meet. Roger Weil was one of the first to minister behind the Iron Curtain when the Cold War was still in deep freeze—smuggling Bibles, typewriters, and training materials; teaching; encouraging; and helping. Beneath the meticulous manner of an English gentleman, Roger is an old warrior still very much in the arena. He came to Christ as a college student over fifty years ago under the powerful preaching of Dr. Martyn Lloyd-Jones. It was Roger's first visit to Westminster Chapel, and the text was "the Son of man is not come to destroy men's lives, but to save them" (Luke 9:56 KJV). Last night Roger recounted for me the convicting, convincing power of the Word. Though over half a century has passed since that day, his eyes glistened with tears of joy to tell it—as one who had touched the hem of Christ's garment.

This morning we whisked southward from Victoria Station through a late winter countryside dotted with sheep and blushing with spring color. In just under an hour, we were looking over a gray English sea and walking on what, in missions history, is sacred ground. Here on Brighton Beach, Hudson Taylor made the decision from which the China Inland Mission was born. Not only did the mission become the greatest single force in the evangelization of China in the nineteenth century and the first half of the twentieth, but it also provided a model for many other organizations that would penetrate into other unreached lands in Asia and Africa.

Brighton Beach

Along the way, Roger helped me understand the big picture of that long-ago day on Brighton Beach, where prayer turned to peace, vision to action. Years ago when Roger made risky trips behind the Iron Curtain to help pastors and smuggle Bibles and typewriters, God gave him an inexplicable peace that he was with him. A man said to Roger once, "I want to serve Christ in such places, but I can't. I'm afraid." Roger said, "Can you walk on water?" Meaning, the apostle Peter walked on water because he trusted the One who called him to step out into an impossible situation. It reminded me that Peter, Hudson, Roger, and *all* men and women of faith walk on water when they venture all on Christ. Hudson Taylor once observed, "All God's giants have been weak men who did great things for God because they reckoned on His being with them."[3]

Often when we read about "God's giants," we read history

backward. Our heroes stride across the stage of their generation, every decision drawn by the compass of destiny to their rising star. Even defeats, we know, are just a prelude to the victories that will come a few pages later. But that's *reading* history, not *living* it. I thought of that as I walked in the now-famous footsteps of Hudson Taylor along Brighton Beach. To those who know the story, Taylor's decision at Brighton was a tipping point; but in 1865, Hudson Taylor was misunderstood and ridiculed. He lacked formal theological training, and the piecemeal medical studies that he took to help gain initial entrance into China would barely qualify him to ride in the back of an ambulance today. His belief that men and single women could serve Christ on the foreign field was considered by some as dangerous—or worse, scandalous. His conviction that an agency could draw workers together in common cause from different denominations and raise financial support from God's people through prayer alone was considered naive at best.

Because Taylor wanted to lay aside any nonessential barrier to the gospel, he insisted on looking as much as possible like the people he was reaching. This meant not only donning a robe and slippers but also wearing dark glasses to mask his Occidental eyes, dyeing his blond hair black, and having a faux ponytail woven into his hair beneath a silk cap. This man was serious about the getting rid of barriers to the gospel. Many of his colleagues, though, thought he was a nut. Despite the snickers that followed him, those who knew Hudson Taylor knew two things about him. First, no one to that point had taken the gospel further into China's unreached interior than he had. And second, when Hudson Taylor prayed, he got results.

By the time of Brighton, Hudson Taylor had survived nearly seven years of difficult ministry in China, but nothing in China compared to the physical, emotional, and spiritual battle in which he was now engaged at home in England. He saw the need and the neglect of China. "Can the Christians of England sit still with folded arms while these multitudes are perishing?" he wrote. "What does the Master teach us? Is it not that if one sheep out of a hundred be lost, we are to leave the ninety and nine and seek that one? But here the proportions are almost reversed, and we stay at home with the one sheep, and take no heed to the ninety and nine perishing ones! Christian Brethren, think of the imperative command of our great Captain and Leader, 'Go, go ye, into *all* the world, and preach the gospel to *every* creature.'"[4]

By the spring of 1865, the burden had grown acute. As the months wore on, so did the weight of the crisis—the crisis of, in his words, "a million a month" in China dying without Christ. He rarely slept more than a couple of hours at a time, and he was physically and emotionally exhausted. A friend invited him to come to the seaside for a weekend to get away and to get perspective.

On Sunday morning, June 25, 1865, Taylor heard a stirring message from the Presbyterian preacher J. M. Denniston. Then, as he wrote later:

> Unable to bear the sight of a congregation of a thousand or more Christian people rejoicing in their own security, while millions were perishing for lack of knowledge, I wandered out on the sands alone, in great spiritual agony; and there the Lord conquered my unbelief, and I surrendered myself to God for this service. I told Him that all the responsibility as to the issues and consequences must rest with Him; that as His servant it was mine to obey and to follow Him—His to direct, to care for, and to guide me and those who might labour with me. Need I say that peace at once flowed into my burdened heart? There and then I asked Him for 24 fellow workers, two for each of eleven inland provinces which were without a missionary, and two for Mongolia.[5]

There, with the sea breeze catching the pages of his Bible, he opened to his reading for that day, Job 18, and wrote on the top margin: "Prayed for 24 willing, skilful labourers, Brighton, June 25/65." Afterward he wrote, "Felt as if I could fly up that hill by the station . . . how I did sleep that night! Mrs. Taylor thought that Brighton had done wonders! And so it had."[6]

Today I retraced Hudson Taylor's steps on Queens Road, where he dashed up from the beach. If he walked it now, he would pass Big Bites Fish & Chips and would have picked up his pace as he reached Boots Midnight Pharmacy, where the hill begins its rise. If he successfully dodged the double-decker buses that ply this road, perhaps he would have crossed Queens between the all-you-can-eat Chinese buffet and Mr. Topper's barbershop. He would have also passed the church he walked out of in 1865—it's still standing but is now gutted and shuttered.

Here in front of the Flying Bean Cappuccino Stand, where I grabbed a cup before catching the train back to London, I like to think of Hudson Taylor stepping off the curb with a light heart. He has no time for coffee though—he has a continent to conquer! But I like to think of him this way because it reminds me that God does not work only in a black-and-white tintype world of the past.

So where are our Brightons today? Who are the next Hudson Taylors? Where are the men and women who will venture all on Christ? Perhaps she just passed me on the street. Or perhaps he just stepped off the curb next to the Flying Bean, his steps now ordered by the Lord.

SHENYANG, CHINA

The city is up early, and so am I. From my window I see bundled forms leaning against the wind. We are on the edge of a huge dust storm that's kicking up out of the Gobi Desert. The sun is just a red smudge on the thick sky.

Met last night in room 603 on the backside of the Jin Jiang hotel. The room was crowded with men and women reporting from the front. One of them was Wuzhou, who goes by Joseph, a house church leader in Shenyang. Last year he was copying and distributing ten thousand copies of the JESUS film. But the operation was too big, and the police caught him. Perhaps because he is the son of a Communist official, he got off light—just a huge fine, the equivalent of a year's wages! Joseph seemed to take it in stride. In fact, he said nothing of this—I learned it from others. Rather, he is looking ahead, focused on strengthening the more than three hundred believers in the house church here in the city, which more recently broke up into numerous cell groups. As Uncle Zhao reminded us, "It is easier to strike an eagle than ten sparrows."

Dear Uncle Zhao. "Uncle" is the common term among Chinese Christians for an older leader, a patriarch. Because of a mutual friend, I was able to meet with him. As we talked on into the night, Uncle shared how he came to Christ as a boy nearly seventy years ago. He told of the awful pressures upon believers in the 1950s and '60s and about the darkest days of Mao's Cultural Revolution. Once during that time Zhao was put to the test. Forced to stand before a portrait of Mao, he was ordered to say, "Long live Mao!" Overcome from fear for himself and his wife and children, he did it. But then he was pressed to deny Christ, to denounce God. This he would not do. The men beat him, fracturing his ribs, cheekbone, and breaking his back in two places. Dear Uncle, like the apostle Paul, can say, "I bear on my body the marks of Jesus" (Gal. 6:17).

Later, a friend let Zhao in on a dangerous secret—a shortwave radio. Uncle would lie out in the fields at night and listen to Voice of America broadcasts. It awakened, or better to say the Lord awakened, a ridiculously impossible dream in the heart of this beaten, badgered man hiding in a field in the dark: that he should provide a voice for Christ for the scattered house churches of China. But how? "With man it is impossible, but not with God" (Mark 10:27). From his hiding place in some dark rice field, Zhao could only look up.

Several years passed, but the dream did not. Zhao was able to escape China with his family, and then began what would become a twenty-year radio ministry to the Chinese house church with broadcasts beamed in from nearly every side. To house church leaders without training, commentaries, or even Bibles, Uncle Zhao's daily messages were heard, repeated, and repeated again, as they rippled across China. Known by voice to millions, he now travels all over China under different names. In fact, not long ago he was in Xinjiang in the far western borderland where the old Silk Road cuts between the desert of Tarim Pendi and the rugged ranges of Tian Shan. Millions live there, and the government is encouraging more to move. Some Christian families have joined the migration, and others are preparing to go, farm, and evangelize—and Uncle Zhao was there to strengthen the fledgling churches on China's final frontier.

We talked until nearly midnight, rejoiced together, prayed together, embraced, and parted into the night. Uncle had to keep moving—and so do we.

Gateway to the Forbidden City

BEIJING, CHINA

I've ducked into a nearby Starbucks to write and to warm up. A dark wind is sweeping over Beijing, and the dust storm is spreading southward. Tiananmen Square is nearly deserted. A massive portrait of Mao oversees one end of the great square, but there is little to see—just a few detachments of the People's Army and the hardier tourists. Mao's portrait hangs over the ancient gateway that enters the outer courtyards of the Forbidden City—the sprawling, splendid imperial residence. "Forbidden" because it was closed to the outside world. Like China and her great cities today, it, too, is no longer forbidden. The Communist facade remains, but Christ is building his church here, and neither the gates of hell nor of Mao can prevail against it.

SOMEWHERE WEST OF BEIJING

Mr. Zhang, our taxi driver, is certainly an animated fellow—at times gesturing with both hands while careening through head-on traffic. We are in search of a "secret" baptismal service of a house church in Beijing. We have vague directions—take the road west, pass the apple orchard, follow bus 727 to a bridge . . .

Even though we are well outside Beijing, the air is still thick and hazy—and the sun is never seen. The swirling dust is relieved only by an occasional broken water line filling the cratered road with mud. Men with leather faces squat alongside the road roasting ears of corn on open fires, piling stacks of black, sooty husks all around them.

Mr. Zhang has stopped once again, offering cigarettes in exchange for directions, which thus far have been conflicting, but the bridge here looks promising. We got out at the bridge, walking down a dirt road that wound along the Ye Xi River. When we rounded a bend, we heard the singing of "Amazing Grace," and what we saw was also amazing—hundreds standing beneath the willows along the river bank. About two hundred people were in line to be baptized, and more were arriving! At least that many more were there to share in this time of witness and worship. Morning mist still clung to the river, where the pastors stood and received one believer after another from the long line. The old pastor of the church, the venerable Allen Yuan, sat with his wife, and they laid hands on and prayed for each person being baptized. Pastor is ninety years old and has spent twenty-three years in prison for his faith, including torture during the days of Mao.

For a moment there, standing on the banks of that misty river, I wasn't sure if I was in the twenty-first century or the first century!

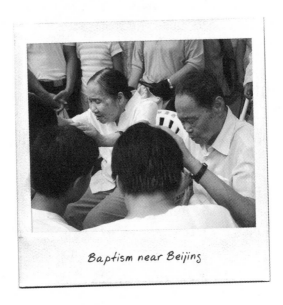

Baptism near Beijing

ON THE RAIL TO XIAN, CHINA

Before the lights go out, I'll scribble a few lines. We departed Beijing at 4:50 p.m. from the massive West Terminal for the beginning of our two-thousand-mile journey by train through the Chinese heartland and to the western borderlands.

Because of fear of unrest among ethnic (mostly Muslim) minorities in the west, the Chinese government keeps a closer watch on Christian activity there, and foreigners get added scrutiny. And so, for our journey to the far western province of Xinjiang, beyond the Great Gobi, we have turned ourselves into a multinational, camera-snapping tour group. Along with friends from Singapore and America, David has come over from Albania, and my son has joined us, too. Tim Jr. is a good traveler with a quick ear for Mandarin and a winning way with people. Chun-Yan, our Chinese tour guide, is a dear, brave sister. She has a number of contacts she will introduce us to among the underground Christian leaders in the west. Some of these are friends of friends, and some she has spent time with in a jail cell.

We have a second-class compartment, and apart from the squat toilets, it's clean. The bunks are in groups of six and open to the aisle, which is packed with passengers and odors. We took our supper in the dining car, where we enjoyed a variety of dishes, such as pork and leeks, fresh fish, and spicy donkey meat. We talked for a while, but as our train jostles southward into the night, sleep is claiming us one by one. Our train arrives in Xian at six in the morning. With the lights, security checks, foot traffic, and these open berths, sleep is doubtful, but I'm ready to try.

XIAN, CHINA

I am sitting in a smoky Internet café waiting for Tim Jr. and David to finish sending messages back home. A steady rain is falling outside on the crowded streets of Xian. We arrived in this ancient city at first light. Old and proud, like the ranks of the crinkled matriarchs I saw doing their morning tai chi, Xian was once the great city of a great tyrant two centuries before Christ was born. The emperor Qin Shi Huang was both a builder and destroyer. The Great Wall was one of his projects. A million peasant prisoners were conscripted to build it, and thousands of them, dead from exhaustion, were buried in it like human mortar.

After a quick Chinese breakfast, we set out to see Qin Shi Huang's other great project—his Great Tomb with its army of terracotta warriors. I wasn't prepared for the scale of it—seven thousand soldiers, horses, and archers arrayed in ranks marching from their underworld graves after two thousand years. Each figure is painstakingly reconstructed, a process that can take archeologists up to three months each—so, slowly, more and more of these soldiers rise from the earth. There is also a great bronze chariot of exquisite craftsmanship to transport the emperor's soul into the next world, where he would enjoy the power and splendor he had known in this life: untold treasure, one hundred concubines, plus dancers, musicians, and even a grand army to command and protect his palace pleasures. Yet it was nothing but futility on an enormous scale—just like the Great Wall that never kept back China's invaders, so Qin Shi Huang's tomb city never gave him everlasting life. In the end, he died like the thousands who lost their lives building his monumental follies.

It's an interesting irony that the great emperor burned all of the records of previous rulers, as if nothing existed before him, yet he and his tomb were forgotten, tramped underfoot by others' histories—and plows. The tomb was discovered about forty years ago, as some peasants were digging a well and discovered this cavernous crypt. One of these farmers (a Mr. Yang) is still around and something of a local celebrity. He was in the gift shop today signing autographs between long drags on his pipe. I felt a little sorry for him. He seemed awkward, like he would rather be planting rice than drawing his name on postcards. Old Mr. Yang is just another peasant-prisoner to the emperor's grandeur—the last of many.

LANZHOU, GANSU PROVINCE, CHINA

Arrived in this Silk Road city this morning by train from Yinchuan. A brother named Wei and his wife Xue met us at the train station. For us they go by "Samuel" and "Grace." They were sent west as missionaries from house churches in the northeast of China. I've read of such Chinese missionaries, but Sam is the first one I've met. He and Grace came to Lanzhou by train from Heilongjiang on the Russian border—a fifty-eight-hour train ride on "hard seats" (the cheapest) with a great desire to reach people for Christ, especially young people, and challenge them and train them to serve the Lord.

Today we saw the whole spectrum of religion in Lanzhou. This morning we climbed a mountain overlooking this sprawling city, which is the gateway to the Gobi and the West. There was a pagoda on the face of the mountain. The path leading us there was a series of steep switchbacks, and with temperatures at about 100°, by the time we reached the Buddhist temple, the air was graced with a mixture of sweat and sweet incense. There were various images of the Buddha around a central brazier of fire and incense. One of the images was of the "sleeping Buddha," who seemed quite indifferent to both the penitents bowing low before him in a cloud of incense and to the bird droppings on his flaking gold face. The whole sad scene was one of the utter emptiness of idolatry.

Afterward we went to a huge new mosque in Lanzhou, which was funded by the Saudis. When we walked up to the courtyard, the men were just coming out of the mosque from noon prayer. Most did not seem pleased to see us. I realized that some people here have never seen a Westerner in person, but for some of these Muslims, there was more than surprise behind the sneers. One man stopped my Chinese friend and demanded, "Are these Americans or British?" He refused to answer. The man then got in our face and said, "Osama bin Laden is my hero. 9/11 and the London bombings made me happy." Then baring his teeth he said, "You are not welcome here!" This devout Muslim had just gotten up from his prayers and declared that the killing of thousands of innocent men, women, and children made him "happy." Ironically, while this man was spewing his hatred for Americans and British people, the children of the imams were running around and eagerly practicing their English on us.

Late this afternoon we strolled along the muddy Yellow River and visited a nearby Taoist temple. Taoism combines the most ancient Chinese superstitions into one miserable dungeon of the damned. Fortune-tellers cluttered the walkway between card tables piled with incense sticks and huge stacks of "hell money"—special paper money to be burned for the dead on the temple altar. Stepping inside, it was in fact like a little hell. Smoke was rising from an ashen brazier before a golden demon image. The temple master, his brown, furrowed face twisted like an old root, did not want us there. The Spirit of Christ dwelling in us was not welcome in this den of demons. Even as I write, a heavy sense of sadness still comes over me when I think of those poor lost people there in that temple of doom. The place and the people are so close to hell.

Today we saw religion, but tonight we caught a glimpse of Christ through the joyful testimonies of Samuel's mom and dad—Sister Sung and Brother Kao. For thirty years they have served the Lord and led many to the Savior. Their testimonies were told with tearful joy because, as Sister Sung put it, "the love of God gripped me"— and clearly he has not let her go.

Over the years, Sister Sung and Brother Kao witnessed far and wide and started house churches in Dun Jiang, Mulan, and the Black River region, but the fires of persecution have followed them. Yet like the three Hebrew children, the fire did not consume them, and they found Christ with them in the midst.

Once the police raided the church at Dun Jiang. The police chief denounced the Christians as being part of a "capitalist dog religion," and with threats of criminal charges, he and his henchmen began days of interrogations. However, little did the chief know that his wife was a "lady Nicodemus," secretly meeting at night with Sister Sung to know more about Christ. She believed on the Lord Jesus—and then openly declared him. Her witness to her husband ended the investigation—and eventually led him to the Savior.

In another city, a police spy planted in a house church came under conviction after hearing testimonies of men with notorious pasts. As a police officer, he had beaten and tortured men for their crimes, but that had not stopped them from stealing or fighting. How is it that the gospel has the power to *change* a person? Under deep conviction, he soon found out for himself!

Another man was sick, and as a superstitious Taoist, he sought help from seers. He went to one renowned fortune-teller in the city, but the man had recently become a Christian. His advice to him now was, "You need the Lord!" Surprised and disappointed over this "fortune," he sought out another fortune-teller, but he too had been converted and advised the sick man, "You need the Lord!" This man went to five fortune-tellers—all of whom had come to Christ. Upon their witness, he found that Christ was indeed his true fortune.

All of these testimonies were reminders that the gospel "is the power of God for salvation" (Rom. 1:16) and that "the weapons of our warfare are not of the flesh but have divine power to destroy strongholds" (2 Cor. 10:4). We parted about midnight with prayer, a song, and much joy.

CROSSING THE GOBI DESERT

The Xinjiang train rumbles along through the northern Gansu. Dusk hangs over the brown expanse that slips by, and everyone in our crowded train is settling in for the night. My bed on the top of a six-bunk compartment is coffin-like—just two feet high and wide. Fortunately, it is open at the end so my feet can stick into the aisle, which is filled with people eating strange, pungent foods. One man near me is eating something that resembles nightcrawlers and washing them down with beer. Then again, several fellow travelers were repulsed by my supper. Tim Jr. and I made up some peanut butter and jelly sandwiches and were savoring every bite, having been away from such fine fare for several weeks. We looked up to find passengers gathered around staring with curiosity and horror at what pale people eat!

Tim Jr. is now in the next train car, probably practicing his Chinese on curious bunkmates. I'll check on him and then try to sleep. By morning we should be in the middle of the Gobi Desert.

WEST OF HAMI, CHINA

Reached the oasis town of Hami about nine in the morning. Took advantage of the quick stop to stretch. Some men at the train station were carrying enormous melons—the Hami melon is said to be the best in China. Where springs are in the desert, the land blossoms—rich corn, sweet melons, and bright sunflowers. But beyond the reach of water, it is bleak, barren, and boundless. The only life to be seen from the train is an occasional herd of brown camels in the brown distance tugging on some brown scrub.

ÜRÜMQI, XINJIANG PROVINCE, CHINA

I am sick again today—actually, I haven't been well for a week but have pushed through. However, today I had to stay behind at our hotel. The English name for it reads "Peafowl Mansions," which would seem to be a translator's near-miss for the Peacock Hotel. However, with the roaches and sewer smells that come up the drain-pipe, I think there must be another meaning to the "fowl" part.

The rest of the team went to visit a Uighur village. I am missing out, but the Lord gave me a good day of fellowship with him. It has been a time of rebuke for my lack of faith and dimness of vision, but it has also been a time of great joy over Calvary love. Even on this day that I am set aside, Christ has given me beauty for ashes because of the cross. As I look out my window on this great city of nearly three million souls, the towers of commerce, the mosques of Islam, and the temples of Buddhism all rise over this city, but where is the cross? In the distance, the snow-capped Bogda Shan ("the mountain of God") dominates the horizon, but who here knows God?

ÜRÜMQI, XINJIANG PROVINCE, CHINA

Writing a few lines before catching some sleep. It has been a long day, a long journey for all of us. Caught a bus to the old bazaar for supper. The bazaar was fascinating, reminiscent of Samarkand, only bigger. The streets and narrow alleys were filled with everything imaginable from clothes to cabbages, kebabs to copper kettles! The crowd numbered in the thousands. Muslim men milled about buying and selling, their caps and long robes denoting their status and tribe. Women with beautiful, curious eyes peered out of the slits in their veils at us strangers, who looked back with equal curiosity. It seemed that we were no longer in China, but rather central Asia. Indeed, this region was known as Turkestan before it was part of China. Uighurs, Kazakhs, Uzbeks, and Tajiks all call this home. The majority Han are more recent arrivals sent over the last fifty years to take greater political and economic control over this vast borderland so that the Uighurs will be a minority in their own region, just as the Tibetans are in Tibet. This migration of Han Chinese to the "Wild West" has also brought the light of the gospel to this remote region—one of the unintended consequences of Mao's effort to dominate the borderlands.

Chun-Yan introduced us to Lan-Lan, a third-generation Christian. Her grandparents were believers who were sent west by the Communists in one of the first waves. House churches emerged wherever such Christians settled as the gospel spread by word of mouth, neighbor to neighbor. Lan-Lan is a joyful reminder that Christ has his people everywhere—even on the far side of the Gobi Desert.

Lan-Lan: Back to Jerusalem

ÜRÜMQI, XINJIANG PROVINCE, CHINA

Reached the westernmost point on our journey. Climbed the mountain pass that led to a place known as Tian Chi—"the Heavenly Lake." The snow-capped peaks that rise beyond it are called "the Heavenly Mountains." In the forest along the way, we had a wonderful time of worship as Lan-Lan sang from her worn, little, handwritten hymnbook. She sang songs of praise, songs of the cross, and a song of advance—"Back to Jerusalem." This missionary hymn is the heartbeat of the Chinese church—to continue the gospel's course westward. The gospel that was first preached "beginning at Jerusalem" nearly two thousand years ago, went to Europe, then to the Americas, later to China, and now they will take the light of Christ westward to Islam's darkest lands—all the way "Back to Jerusalem." For cross-bearers like Lan-Lan, Samuel, Grace, Chun-Yan, and many others who have taken this path, it is a staggering vision that may demand everything of them—both life and death.

After Lan-Lan finished singing, we continued our climb toward "the Heavenly Mountains." The Lord was gracious to remind us of his power and promises. We reached a waterfall of the clearest water, deafening in its force. The mist fell over us and, in the bright sun, caught us in a prism of rainbow light, as an eagle soared high above. It was as if the words of Isaiah were written in the sky:

> They shall mount up with wings like eagles;
> they shall run and not be weary;
> they shall walk and not faint. (Isa. 40:31)

BAOTOU, INNER MONGOLIA, CHINA

Arrived in Baotou late morning. Baotou hugs the banks of the Yellow River here in the Mongolian plateau, and at 2.6 million, it is the largest city in this province.

Met a young lady named Altantsetseg, which means "golden flower." Mongolians do not have surnames, and her name is that of the bright yellow wildflowers that deck the grasslands here. Mercifully for our uncooperative tongues, we can call her by her adopted English name, Alice. Alice is working in campus evangelism and discipleship in Dalian. She made a thirty-hour train ride here to accompany our little team across her homeland of Inner Mongolia and to introduce us to Christians along the way. Tonight before our prayer time, Alice shared how she came to faith in Christ, and with joy she sang songs of praise in the Mongolian tongue. The sound was sweet and clear. A winsome loneliness clung to its rhythms, like the companionship of the wind that only a Mongolian shepherdess could know. What a day that will be when Mongolian voices join the choir from every tribe and nation, all of us singing praise to the Lamb that was slain!

Our bus rumbles on through the Yellow River valley near Baotou. Here a thin skin of green sheaths the land, but beyond the reach of water, it is all sand and scrub. We had a good time in the desert riding camels among the dunes and enjoying a good Mongolian meal—spicy mutton and delicious grass-like greens called desert onions. The pig ears were a bit waxy but had a nice crunch! There were many other dishes—all quite tasty but of unknown origin.

It is a drowsy drive back. Many on the bus are slumped over, catching rubber-neck naps. But Alice is busy talking with our tour guide, Wu-Wen, sharing Christ with her. Alice delights to shine for Christ and speak of him.

HOHHOT, INNER MONGOLIA, CHINA

After a late supper at the end of a long day, I am trying to catch up on some writing. We just returned from a Mongolian meal served at a restaurant with greasy tables arranged beneath a grimacing portrait of Genghis Khan. The thick air was mixed with cigarettes and steamy Hohhot hot pot, but we found the food to be quite good. In the cramped upper room where we ate, it was a respite—a time to sit and talk over all we have heard and seen today.

The best news of the day was that Wu-Wen accepted Christ as her Savior. She had first heard the gospel last summer at an English camp, but Alice's faithful witnessing brought her to understanding and decision. Praise the Lord for my new sister!

More and more like Wu-Wen are coming into the kingdom across Inner Mongolia, from the cities to the grasslands. In little more than a year the church in the area has grown to over one thousand. They meet in ten house churches—some in the city, some among the shepherds on the prairie. In another town, the house church meets in the home of a seamstress named Nashso. A brother named Amrad took me over to Nashso's house, where she eagerly took out from beneath her mending her treasured copy of the Mongolian Bible.

Six months ago Nashso's husband divorced her, abandoning her and their eight-year-old son. As she walked out of the court where she was given divorce notification—overwhelmed by hopelessness—she met a Christian who shared the good news that she too had only recently heard and believed. Nashso trusted Christ right there. She said, "The worst day of my life became the best day of my life!"

The group of believers that gather in her cramped apartment has grown from four to forty in six months. "Who is the preacher?" I asked. "Whoever has a Bible." "Do you know how to preach?" "No, I just know how to read the Bible." "How did the church grow so quickly?" "I don't know, they just come!"

These people don't even know the terms "church planting" or "soul winning," they just know that *Isus Hkristus* (Jesus Christ) has given them new life—and the news is too good to keep! The gods they once served and feared are no more than they appear—just wood and stone. So it is Acts in action, lived out in marvelous ignorance of methods and machinery, as the wind of the Spirit sweeps over these Mongolian plains.

IN A YURT NEAR SHANGDU, INNER MONGOLIA, CHINA

I finished out my last day on the Mongolian plains in a fitting way—on a horse. And the horse had spirit! He kicked his handler when he brought him out of the corral, and when I rode him he took all the rein I would give him. These are the plains that Marco Polo crossed seven centuries ago. This afternoon we explored fields where he lived long ago and saw the ruins of the great city he once described, known then as Xanadu, which opened Europe's thirst for exploration. The old columns now lay fallen among bright wildflowers.

Near our yurt stands a perfect cone of a hill. On its peak is an *ao-bao*—a pile of stones. Such altars were raised long ago by Mongol shamans as a place of prayer and sacrifice to their gods of fear and bondage. We climbed this one today to seek the face of the only true God to pray for the gospel to continue to shake this land and for the day when crosses would be raised over these high places. In Mongolian and English, we pleaded for these people for whom Christ died. There on the summit's immense pile of stones, where bleached bones lay and the wind played among the faded shreds of silk prayer banners, we prayed for the day when Christ's glory would be known throughout the land!

SHENYANG, CHINA

A cold rain is falling, veiling the sea of cranes and scaffolded towers of a rising city. From my apartment window, I watched the poor, weary workers from the nearby construction site retreat for shelter under an eave. Sleep-hungry, they lay in crumpled piles, looking so much like heaps of lost luggage.

These sturdy farm boys with their hard hands, sun-darkened faces, and bemused stares at pale Westerners are pouring into the cities looking for work and fueling China's engine. Others are coming to the city, too—not for construction work but for college. And so, ironically, just forty years after Mao's madness—the Cultural Revolution—with its reckless, bloody assault on education, the past is paved over with glittering new campuses. In fact, these nap-snatching workers are building a high-rise fine arts center over the grave of a village that was thriving when I first came here only five years ago.

China is rushing the future—its rise rapid and impressive. Yet there is another power rising that is more impressive still—Christ's kingdom. It is estimated that there are nearly one hundred million Christians in China. Here among our brothers and sisters, their vision is rising to the occasion. Just a few years ago, the local house church here was reaching two campuses—now it is reaching twenty-two! And these house churches have increased tenfold as well. The men who shepherd them seem tireless—operating "beneath the radar," they are given to evangelism, discipleship, and now missions beyond their city. Their kingdom-dreams are as big as China!

I met with one campus leader yesterday. He only recently believed and has already led over thirty of his classmates to Christ—and is also reaching a neighboring campus as well. Another believer, Li Yun, despite occasional trips to the police station for questioning, goes room to room in the dorms and asks, "Are you a Christian?" and shares the gospel with any who will listen. The gospel is shared as it was received—boldly, joyfully, and expectantly. For them, this is normal Christianity. And so Christ's kingdom grows across China, just as Isaiah said it would: "Behold, you shall call a nation that you do not know, and a nation that did not know you shall run to you, because of the LORD your God" (Isa. 55:5).

Looking over this sea of cranes and spindly scaffolds, I recall something Hudson Taylor wrote from this land after his Brighton Beach experience: "The Lord is prospering us, and the work is steadily growing, especially in that most important department, native help. . . . the future hope for China lies, doubtless, in them. I look on foreign missionaries as the scaffolding round a rising building; the sooner it can be dispensed with the better—or rather, the sooner it can be transferred to other places, to serve the same temporary purpose."[7]

Hudson Taylor's dream is coming true. The scaffolding is coming down, a building is rising. "This is the LORD's doing; it is marvelous in our eyes" (Ps. 118:23).

4
WITHIN A YARD OF HELL

Southeast Asia

Island hopping: near the Sulu Sea

Lonely Planet guidebooks and the picture postcards thrust in your face at every tourist trap show the pretty places—golden palaces, fields of glistening green rice, mysterious temples, and smiling people. Here in the knot of nations in the southeast corner of Asia, there is much more behind the mask.

In parts of the region, war has claimed more than seven million lives in the past generation. Though the old battlefields are being planted and paved over, scars remain. Cambodia has the distinction of having more landmine amputees per capita than any other country. In Vietnam and Laos, the legacy of Communism can be found in repressive regimes, the persecution of Christians, and fifty-eight thousand American soldiers' graves. But the problems are much deeper than old wars and dead dictators. Drug lords and slave traders are the new masters of misery. Girls and boys are being sold to sex traffickers for as little as twenty dollars. They are "throwaway" kids—abused, addicted, and often dead from AIDS before they even grow up. Besides all this, the stultifying darkness of Buddhism and animism has held sway for centuries—religion that is no more than fear of idols, of demons, of the dead.

Yet, such darkness is no match for the light of the gospel. Here's one example. It comes from JD Crowley, a pioneer missionary who serves among the Tampuan and Krung peoples in the borderlands where Cambodia, Vietnam, and Laos connect. His letter beautifully illustrates the power of the gospel to bring light, deliverance, and spontaneous joy:

> In a few hours I will ride my motorcycle out to the village of Krala and teach the last two of twenty-four Creation to Christ lessons to a group of around twenty Krung Christians and almost-Christians. Most of the teaching has been done by locals, but I've had the privilege of teaching a few myself, and the response has been encouraging.
>
> After I taught on the Ten Commandments, a middle-aged man said, "I've broken every one of these commandments many, many times; how can I possibly be reconciled to God?" Others nodded their heads as if to say that they were wondering the same thing. In twelve years here, I've never had anyone ask me that question or seem to be under so much conviction.
>
> I skipped ahead and gave them a short explanation about the Lamb of God who took away the sins of the world on the cross. They actually started clapping and praising God spontaneously, as if a great burden had been lifted. It was a perfect example of God's law preparing people for God's grace. I believe that some came into the kingdom right then and there as the light went on in their hearts and minds.
>
> The Krung preacher who was supposed to do today's final lessons is ill, and the great privilege has fallen on me to teach about

the death of Christ, and the resurrection and ascension. Please pray for the power of the Holy Spirit to be on us, that the little bamboo house on the edge of Krala would be the Holy of Holies today. Pray that this stronghold of the Enemy would become a village filled with believers. Every square inch of Krala village belongs to our Lord Jesus Christ. Let's claim it for his glory![1]

The same could be said of every unreached corner of Southeast Asia and of the world—every square inch belongs to our King!

KOH KONG, CAMBODIA

I'm writing to pass a restless night. From my balcony, the sea breeze feels good, sweeping over now-empty streets. Only Orion is keeping vigil.

Took Highway 3 from Bangkok to Trat this morning, and then skirted along the Gulf of Thailand to cross into Cambodia. A six-hour drive that took us, it seemed, past a hundred dusty towns displaying the usual fading portraits of their king and a Buddhist temple as the centerpiece. Our driver, a kindly man named Nu, was careful to clasp his hands and give a quick nod of obeisance as we passed the gilded shrines with their garish gods—drive-by worship at sixty miles per hour!

In one town I noticed a man making idols out of concrete, while nearby a concrete mixer was being used to patch the road. But this land is in the bondage of Buddhism, and so the people are as blind to such ironies as the gods of cement that they worship.

Crossed the border at Cham Yeam, a notorious crossing used mostly by smugglers and addicts. A casino and a string of tawdry hotels sit alongside the border station, making it convenient for sex traffickers, drug addicts, and pedophiles that come here on "business trips."

Reached Koh Kong early this afternoon, where I met up with a Filipino couple, Noe and Grace. Noe pastors a church here, and they run a children's home to the south near Sihanoukville. But mostly, they act as the hands of Jesus, picking up "throwaway" kids from the streets and dumps, loving those with AIDS, and reaching those snared and stained by the sex trade. This is a labor of love—a labor of Calvary love.

After a quick lunch, we discussed the AIDS situation in this city. Koh Kong has the highest rate of AIDS of any province in Cambodia—there are eight thousand known cases, and many are children. They are cared for in two places, if "care" is the word for it. Those in the early stages, as well as the AIDS orphans, stay at a Buddhist temple. Those in the late stages are sent to a nearby hospital. Of course, these places only treat a fraction of people with AIDS. Most people come and get their death sentence diagnosis, get some medicine, and then are sent home to suffer and die. Prostitutes continue to work for food and thus spread the disease further.

Noe called the doctor to see what the pressing needs were right now and was told that the patients needed something to eat. So we bought a supply of food and took it to them. The "hospital" is more of a place to go and die. Cattle graze on the grounds, and dogs wander freely through the wards. Families of the patients stay with them to cook and care for them. It broke my heart to see a mother with AIDS point out her daughter—a beautiful, young girl—perhaps like her mom was once. Now the mother is just a skeleton. When I put my arm around her before we prayed, I felt only bones beneath sweat-stained clothes that clung to her. What can I say as I look into these pitiful, hopeless faces as they slip into the grave? What could I say? So I prayed. *God, your Word is more than my words. Through Christ, give life to them before they die. Take away their shame because Christ has already taken it all upon himself, so they might stand before you unashamed, covered in his righteousness.* Grace translated so that they could understand my prayer in their Khmer tongue.

Afterward, I visited the Buddhist temple where AIDS victims and orphans are being cared for. The Buddhist monk in charge was very appreciative of our visit and of the food we brought for the sick. I was quietly rebuked by his example. Yes, we brought a few meals for these people, but he cares for these modern-day lepers day after day after day. Most Christians are afraid of dirty, dying people. How is it that a lost Buddhist monk surpasses Christians in showing compassion for people for whom Christ died?

Waiting to die:
AIDS hospital in Koh Kong

KOH KONG, CAMBODIA

We set out this morning early from Koh Kong. The moon was setting and the sun rising as we walked to the docks and hired a boat for a couple of bucks for the crossing to the little island of Bang Kachang. The houses on the island are built on stilts to accommodate high tide. All of the garbage and sewage goes into the water, leaving the little island afloat in filth. The kids live and play in the water or mud—and malaria, dysentery, and typhoid take their toll.

Marie, a Filipina missionary here, gathered the kids for their Bible club—an amazing permission has been given by the chief on this Buddhist island. The rest of us met with the village leaders to discuss the needs of the school—clean water and a library. Both of these projects are definitely doable. Not only will it help the kids, but it will help keep the door open for gospel outreach on this crowded little island.

We took the boat back in time for a late Sunday morning service in Koh Kong. Noe is a very animated preacher. He preached from Psalm 1:3, "He is like a tree planted by streams of water," which is a lot like his ministry strategy among the young people in Cambodia. It is a strategy of long-term loving and leadership development.

Noe and Grace pour their lives into the lives of these children, and the plants are taking root. Some of them live in the church house, but kids from all over the neighborhood are welcome—not just on Sunday but also after school. They are just kids who, like most kids, like to laugh, sing, play games, and eat sweets; but these little ones also have enormous problems. Many of them get only two meals a day at home. Some have AIDS. One girl has been sent by her mother to sell herself in the red-light district.

The red-light houses are all around the church. I drove around last night to see them, for Koh Kong, as in much of Cambodia, is notorious for child prostitutes and trafficking in young girls. Along dark, muddy roads, red fluorescent lights were strung up in front of shabby bars where girls (some of them no more than children) sit waiting and calling out for customers. These girls become the prey of pedophiles because their parents need the money to feed hungry mouths at home. Here life is cheaper than a meal.

Only the gospel can heal such sick sin; so the church in Koh Kong is well situated among the red lights and dark paths. It's like the words of the pioneer missionary, C. T. Studd, "Some want to live within the sound of church or chapel bell; I want to run a rescue shop within a yard of Hell."[2]

SOMEWHERE IN WESTERN CAMBODIA

Got an early start with Noe and Grace. We are bound for Sihanoukville on Cambodia's southern coast. A saffron sun was barely clearing the Cardamom Mountains as we turned out of Koh Kong onto a road that's not on any map. As it turned out, the barriers and roadblocks we squeezed past were there for a reason. One day, this road will be paved, bridges will span the rivers, and people will fill up this remote western corner of Cambodia. But for now, it's a trail, a red rut that snakes through the lush, green jungle and ends at a ferry crossing on a nameless river. I'm waiting at the fourth and final ferry crossing today. At these river crossings, ragged, Wild West towns hug the bank, where on both sides concrete and rebar are rising out of the river—a sign of things to come.

I notice that much of the construction work is being done by women—"Rosie the Riveter" types who can bend steel and build bridges. These bridges, though, will sink the ferry business. Indeed, when the spans are complete, this backwater way of life will be swept away like so much water under the bridge. That will be sad, I think, for I love its sounds, smells, tastes, and its people.

The hum of the ferry engine wafts across the river. I hear the clank of the chains of the roustabouts, hoisting the ferry ramp on the farther shore. Women haul up baskets of green mud crabs, still glistening and pawing in the morning light. The crabs, like the scrawny dogs that skulk about the huts, are bound for the dinner pot. The river laps against the raw, red shore. Khmer, Thai, Vietnamese, and Cham mix with the dialect of the river people—the tough locals who, like their shanties, live life on the edge. Girls are scrubbing laundry in the river; and little boys, wearing nothing but a smile, dive off the riverbank and swim as easily as fish do. Stalls covered with old tarps or banana leaves offer travelers every kind of fish and fruit, and, when I am lucky, cans of cold coffee or a fresh coconut. The ferry is nearing our side now—time to move on.

SIHANOUKVILLE, CAMBODIA, ON THE GULF OF THAILAND

The heavy rain has passed, and the sea shimmers in its wake. Slender *tuks* slice the surf as fishermen lean hard into their oars. Boys with an enormous net encircle squid; the squid will be tasty snacks soon, grilled on charcoal spits that blacken the beach here.

We returned from the children's home and from saying good-bye to Noe and Grace. They are doing a wonderful work with the orphans and outcasts that come to them. Some are rag-and-bone children, scavengers who dig for plastic bottles in the garbage. I met two little scavengers—bright, mischievous, twin brothers who are "little" because of malnourishment. All they knew before coming here was gnawing hunger. Noe said that whenever they have testimony time, these boys always stand and say, "I thank God I have food!" Others like Sarie Mei and Joshua had to turn to the street to survive after their father died. When people said they were too hard, too stupid, to learn, Grace said, "That's OK. Give them to me."

Others come full of sores and scars—not just emotional ones, but real scars as well. Ruth's father abandoned her. At just four years of age, she was already staying at the brothel across from her house or sleeping in the street because her stepfather didn't want her. He beat her and even burned her with cigarettes out of cruelty. Ruth's mother eventually gave her to Noe and Grace to raise. Ruth is now a pretty little six-year-old who is finding love for the first time, but when she's alone with her doll, her eyes are very sad.

The Lord Jesus invited children to come to him, and many of these "throwaway" kids have come to Christ because Grace and Noe were his arms to hold them, despite their stench and sores.

PHNOM PENH, CAMBODIA

The sights of the capital. There was the postcard stuff—the golden palaces, the Silver Pagoda, and the National Museum, with its store of ancient buddhas as well as a veritable zoo of idols: the elephant-headed Ganesha, the snake god Naga, and the scowling dog-toothed Yama, god of death. But here in Phnom Penh, where the legacy of the Khmer Rouge years can still be seen, Yama has other monuments, too. Landmine victims were begging for food, dragging their legless bodies along through the muddy litter of the street. This afternoon, I went to Tuol Sleng, Cambodia's Auschwitz. Tuol Sleng was a high school that Pol Pot's goons turned into a prison and torture chamber—the notorious S-21 Unit. That was in the 1970s when the Communist Khmer Rouge committed genocide against their own people. It was a time of insane evil, when as many as two million Cambodians died in the killing fields and, in places like Tuol Sleng, Yama was served well. But comparisons to Nazi death camps fall short. I remember what Robert Kaplan wrote from here not long ago.

> Auschwitz and Dachau had been converted into museums. They had been sanitized by Western curators with heating and air-conditioning, polished-glass display cases, stage lighting, museum shops, and modern toilets for the visiting public. But Tuol Sleng has gone through no such sterilization process. The display cases were crude. It was miserably hot. Rats scavenged in the hallways and wretched toilets. I saw dust balls, spider-webs, and dried blood splattered on the peeling walls. For all I knew, the Khmer Rouge might have left yesterday. The building, with a wire net stretched over the balconies so that torture vic-tims could not commit suicide, had literally been left as it was. The smells of human feces, human sweat, and dead flesh had been erased—that was the only difference. In such a setting, the sight of chains, fingernail and nipple pliers, and photographs of young women with swollen and blackened eyes achieve an effect that you do not find in Europe's particular hells.[3]

I walked through this former high school, where over the space of three years as many as twenty thousand were held and tortured to death. What was especially grievous and insane about the mur-ders at Tuol Sleng was the careful and creative attention given to torture. Death could have been quick—a bullet to the head or, to save precious ammunition, a hoe whack to the skull. But death was not the objective so much as suffering, and to intensify suffering, prisoners were not allowed to cry out—else they were given shocks with an electric cow prod. They would weep but not scream, suf-fering to death in silence.

Looking into the face of her killer

Pol Pot's torturers were careful to photograph all their victims—before and sometimes after being tortured. Many of these photographs were glued to the walls, where once chalkboards hung and students' chatter sounded. The yellowing pictures show mostly youthful prisoners, young men and women looking beyond the camera into the face of their killers. Their expressions vary. For some, their eyes show fear, others defiance or courage, and some show peace. Many Christians were martyred during Pol Pot's bloody rule. Among the hundreds of fading photographs are, no doubt, the faces of saints, God's own children who were to slip from Yama's temple of terror into the everlasting presence of their heavenly Father.

I probably took a hundred pictures of their faces. I don't know why. It seemed that by taking their picture, I could preserve or add some more meaning to their lives. But how do you add meaning to a meaningless death?

The setting sun slanted through the windows, casting the shadows of the prison bars that remain here across the faces of the victims. And for a moment, it seemed that the ghosts of Tuol Sleng stirred.

BANLUNG, RATANAKIRI PROVINCE, CAMBODIA

Took the morning flight from Phnom Penh to Cambodia's rugged northeastern corner of Ratanakiri, where I met missionaries JD and Kim Crowley, who are doing pioneering work in evangelizing the tribal peoples in this remote hill country between Laos and Vietnam. The flight north bumped along rain-laden clouds, often crossing the big, meandering Mekong River, twisting like a big brown snake across the green fields and glistening rice paddies. As we neared Banlung, the clouds lifted for a good view of the jungle cover and the red mud strip that serves as the airport. When JD and I arrived at his home on the outskirts of Banlung, a poor Tampuan woman lay sick on his doorstep. Her name is Sai, and she came with her daughter Chee from the Tampuan village of Patang, nine miles away. We took them to Ratanakiri's only hospital, where JD helped get Sai admitted and treated. Tribal people often have difficulty getting attention from the Khmer. Sai was so weak, her body so light, as we helped her onto the *kray*, a square slat bed. Her "ward" consisted of six *krays* with a couple of twisted wires strung above for mosquito netting. The floor was smeared with mud and bloody bandages, and the strong smell of urine hung in the air. Sai's breathing was shallow and painful. JD suspects typhoid or malaria. At least it's not cholera, which is spreading and killing rapidly in Ratanakiri.

BANLUNG, RATANAKIRI, CAMBODIA

I have crawled under my mosquito netting to pen a few lines before the electricity goes out. The rushing sound of a rain cloud passing through the rubber forest and washing over the coffee grove has passed. The hush is broken only by the patter on the tin roof and the frogs rejoicing in the wet night. For me, too, it is a happy conclusion to a good day.

JD, his son Ethan, and I went out to the *chumka* today. These rice fields are cultivated on the poorer, sloped land that the hill tribes have been forced onto by the Khmer. This time of year—the beginning of the wet season—requires careful attention to the tender rice plants. Therefore, most of the Tampuans stay at the *chumka*, living in thatched huts called *pawk*. We drove as far as the road would take us and then walked a little trail that wound through the dense bush. As we trudged along, forest chickens scrambled under bush and parrots high above called to each other. Here and there along the trail we made quick dashes through rivulets of fire ants crossing our path—unfortunately, Ethan got nipped once, a poisonous sting that lasts two or three minutes.

The trail led through an old forest filled with towering banyan trees with their strange, sinewy trunks and a *koki* tree, which is awesome and Entlike, measuring thirty feet around! The forest ended at a stream, which was deeper, redder, and faster because of monsoon. We carried our boots across and then scrambled up a hill, which opened up into a wide *chumka*. The hillsides were covered with rich, green rice sprouts, set out carefully in rows broken only by an occasional banana tree or charred logs—the remnants of slash-and-burn farming.

I followed JD along paths familiar to him, for these Tampuans are his people, an unreached tribe, that out of love for Christ and these people, JD and Kim and their children have crossed the world to reach. The path through the *chumka* was narrow, and dogs bound for the dinner pot greeted us with a growl; but beyond that, there was a warm welcome from the believers among these families. JD introduced one to me—Lawm, the Fanny Crosby of the Tampuans. Through her blindness, she sees the Savior, and the joy of that brightens her face. Lawm has already composed ten hymns, and now that JD has reduced Tampuan into written form, Lawm's songs form the basis for the first Tampuan book—a hymnal. She invited us to sit on a reed mat with her. I asked her to sing one of her hymns, and after some coaxing, Lawm consented. She sang of light scattering darkness, of freedom in Christ, of him who has untied us from our sin. As she sang, tears trickled from her sightless eyes—and from my eyes, too.

Afterward, JD, Ethan, and I walked about the *chumka*. They have constructed a neat fish trap and pond to help supplement their diet. The fish are fed by shaking termites out of crusty chunks of the huge termite hills that are common here. The Tampuans have no superstitions about termite hills like the Khmer do. Khmer regard them as good luck and even put up little shrines by the termite townhouses! Tampuans regard termites as fish food.

Across one of the streams, a walkway was made from bomb casings of unexploded ordnance from the massive US bombing here along the Ho Chi Minh trail long ago. I noticed one shell had US markings on it, stamped with a February 1970 loading date. The long, green bomb casing is now part of a footbridge, a recycled relic from when war raged over these hills.

Chee at the hospital near Banlung

Afterward JD and I drove back to Banlung and then to the high ground, where upon a weed-choked hill stood a large shrine to the Sleeping Buddha. Rain began to fall, and we found shelter in the pagoda. From our vantage, the valley swirled with rain, and beyond, the mountains of Laos were shrouded in a dark mist. We talked about the unreached peoples of that land and shared some dreams for the work of God in us and through us. JD has such a natural, unaffected walk with Christ, and it is refreshing to talk with him. Sitting there at the feet of the Sleeping Buddha, we prayed to the God who never sleeps. "I lift up my eyes to the hills. From where does my help come? My help comes from the LORD, who made heaven and earth. He will not let your foot be moved; he who keeps you will not slumber" (Ps. 121:1–3).

The sun was drawing the curtain on the day by the time we returned to Banlung. Along the road, children were tugging stubbornly on equally stubborn water buffalo, and families clustered on their *kray*, sharing supper. We had yet one more stop to make. JD wanted to check on Sai and Chee at the hospital. We took some rice, but Sai had no appetite for it. She thinks she wants something sour like green mangoes, but we had none. Sai is still in much pain. It is good that little Chee is with her because there wasn't a doctor or nurse anywhere in the hospital. On the other *kray*, babies with malaria lay on dirty straw mats, and in the courtyard families cooked supper for their sick ones. The wood fires brightened the descending darkness, and the smoke masked the fetid air.

JD and I had a late supper. The bugs are especially numerous and pesky tonight, swirling in the air and crawling all over the table. But thinking about Sai and Chee helps put it all in perspective.

BANLUNG, RATANAKIRI, CAMBODIA

Rained hard most of the day. Standing barefoot in my room this morning, watching the downpour, I looked down in time to see a scorpion about to strike—but I was quicker.

Late afternoon, I sat on the porch and watched what appeared to be a reenactment of the flood, turning muddy roads into muddy rivers. Out of the dense downpour, a man appeared—it was a Tampuan believer name Liu from Patang. He had left the village this morning to bring food to Sai. His motorcycle broke down a mile from home, and he pushed it through the remaining eight miles—

not over a paved road on a pretty day, but rather in a monsoon, mostly along slippery footpaths. Liu's overcoming example of care for a Christian sister is extraordinary and convicting.

PATANG, CAMBODIA

It took an hour and a half to travel the nine miles to the Tampuan village of Patang. The narrow trail through the rubber forest is treacherously slippery during the wet season. We walked the last mile, which descended to the village. The believers gathered from all corners to the church, which is a typical Tampuan house on stilts, ingeniously constructed of split bamboo floors, walls, and roof. They are very sturdy because I am seated with about sixty Tampuans on the lattice floor of bamboo. Besides providing ventilation, the lattice also makes it convenient to spit through, which even the little ones do with great skill!

Hymns were sung with great joy, accented with clapping and drumbeat. The Tampuan drum is a rich, deep mahogany color carved from a single tree. It's hollow at the base, and the head is covered with snakeskin. Prayer is raised in chorus, and testimonies are given with praise for deliverance from evil spirits and the bondage of animal sacrifice. We talked about deliverance and the freedom that Christ gives. A century ago, the Khmer raided this hill country and enslaved their tribal captives. "If someone purchased a captive's freedom," JD asked, "what was it called?" They replied, "Why." (The Tampuan word for redemption is a high, breathy "why.") Many here now know "why."

JD taught a "Creation to Christ" lesson this morning. Afterward most of the folks went back to their *chumka* for the midday meal and rest—some as far as two miles away. JD and I munched on our rice and sardines that Kim had sent along, and washed it down with sweet tea. For dessert, I produced a bag of M&M's, which really delighted JD. We split the bag about eight ways, since we had an audience of village children during the meal. They have no experience with chocolate, so when they tasted the little candy, they said,

"Bitter." It is interesting that our tongues are conditioned to taste the sweet side of chocolate candy. Lacking such experience, they taste the bitter side.

JD strung a hammock for me, tying it to massive bamboo poles, and then left for a time to retrieve the jeep. I stayed behind to rest and write before the afternoon service. A number of the men are taking their rest as well, stretched out on the lattice floor. A few women sit along the wall, holding nursing babies to their breasts. Children are playing in and out of the doorway. One is smoking from a bamboo pipe, and a girl of no more than ten takes long drags from a short stogie of homegrown tobacco, rolled in a green banana leaf.

As the afternoon service drew to a close, so did the day. Sunbeams shown through the bamboo walls and scattered over our circle. It was a perfect picture of what God was doing in this place. "The people who walked in darkness have seen a great light; those who dwelt in a land of deep darkness, on them has light shone" (Isa. 9:2).

The rubber forest was dark and inviting by the time we returned. We stopped briefly to see the waterfall at the Srepok, a river that is one of the Mekong's main tributaries. We reached home and found that Kim had prepared a great supper. It is Father's Day, and since my Sarah and Tim are so far away, the Crowley kids adopted me and included me in their family celebrations tonight.

PHNOM PENH, CAMBODIA

Had my last morning worship with the Crowleys. I opened the Scripture, and JD played his guitar and led in several songs, including one they have taught me since I have been here. It is a theme song of sorts for them. The words are so simple and powerful, and I want it to be my theme as well.

> I want to know Christ and the power of His rising,
> Share in His sacrifice, conform to His death.

As I pour out my life to be filled with His Spirit,
Joy follows suffering, and life follows death.[4]

About noon, JD and I said good-bye to Kim and the kids, and we took a little plane from Banlung to Phnom Penh. There were only ten of us on board, including the governor of Ratanakiri. It was real flying, especially since the pilot inexplicably flew much of the way only about a thousand feet up, skirting over the Mekong, over groves of banana trees, and over palms so close I could count the coconuts. Tonight we are staying in a house near the Chinese embassy. Tomorrow we take a boat up to Siem Reap.

JD Crowley

SIEM REAP, CAMBODIA

What a day! It began early with a motorcycle taxi across Phnom Penh. Hundreds of other motorcycles stream into the streets, where the only rule is speed. JD and I both took motorcycles to the docks near the palace and boarded an old Russian-built riverboat, a rusty leftover from the Vietnam War. We took it up the Tonle Sap River—or more accurately *down* the river, because this time of year the

Tonle Sap reverses course and flows generally northward. It's the only river in the world that does this. During the wet season when the Mekong rises, it pushes the Tonle Sap's southward flow back, forcing it to flow northward, and also enlarges it up to seven times its usual size. With all this movement, the river and its great lake are silt rich—and therefore rich in fish as well.

From Phnom Penh to Kampong Chhnang we passed through the land of the Cham—a proud remnant of Muslims in this land of Buddhism. These Muslims conquered and were conquered centuries ago. Village after village huddled the riverbank. Little boats called *tuk* bobbed in our wake, and scores of children spilled out of the dense bamboo cover to wave and shout greetings. Their fleeting voices were reminders that the gospel story has never been told to the Cham.

After nearly three hours we reached the Tonle Sap Lake, a shallow expanse of water so great that at one point during our crossing we couldn't see a shoreline. Under clear skies, the lake was rich, brown, and frothy—like a sea of cappuccino. JD coaxed the pilot into letting us take turns piloting the boat! All of the instrumentation was, of course, in Cyrillic, and it was in as good a working order as the Soviet Empire, of which the boat is a relic. At any rate, the only "working" boat instrument was the compass. I steered a course northwest across the great lake to a distant peak called Kulen—a blue cone of an ancient volcano.

We anchored well off shore and took a smaller craft to a floating village inhabited by Vietnamese, and then up to Phnom Krom. From there, JD and I took motorcycle taxis the eight miles to Siem Reap. We found a hotel and then continued on by motorcycle another three or four miles to Angkor Wat.

Angkor Wat—only a name in a history book to me until today. The sprawling twelfth-century temple complex defies description. The sheer scale of it exhausts both vocabulary and body to properly gauge it, yet the relief carvings of legends, which cover three-hundred-yard stretches of sandstone wall, are intricate and delicate.

We were having a great time exploring until, unfortunately, JD stumbled in a dark passageway and sprained his ankle very badly—at least I hoped it is only sprained, as it swelled terribly. I helped JD outside the central temple, where a policeman took pity on him and helped get him back to our hotel. JD insisted that I stay longer, and so I did.

This evening when I returned to the hotel room, I found JD propped up on his bed, his ankle packed in ice, and his Bible open, sharing the gospel with two young Khmer men who had helped him back to the room. My driver also joined them, and the three of them sat for nearly an hour listening to the old, old story, which was quite new to them. Sitting there listening, I was struck by how JD takes and makes opportunities to tell about Jesus.

Shortly after the men left, they returned frantic. My driver had lost the key to his motorcycle. We turned the room upside down looking for the little key. I joined the men as we combed through the grass and long, dusty path. The motorcycle was the man's livelihood. The day was waning fast, but we couldn't find the key. We returned to the room and searched again. Finally JD, still propped up with his foot in a bucket of ice, stopped us and said, "Let's pray about this. Let's ask God to help us find the key."

We all knelt down, but my first thought was, "I am not sure this is a good idea. These men are Buddhist. They just heard for the first time in their lives about the one true God. If we don't find the key after we pray, then they will never believe what JD told them about the Lord." I hardly had time to say to myself, "Lord, I believe—help thou mine unbelief," before JD was done praying, making his simple request. When we looked up, the motorcycle man shouted, "I found it! I found the key!" The little key had slipped out of his pocket and down into his shoe, and he saw it when he opened his eyes from praying!

We went right back to prayer, rejoicing in our gracious God who surprised me with his greatness, and who reminded me that prayer is either bound or unbound by my view of him.

It is late now, and light only attracts more lizards; so I will close my chapter on this long day.

ANGKOR THOM, NEAR THE TERRACE OF THE ELEPHANTS, CAMBODIA

Went out early this morning to a clinic that fits landmine victims with artificial limbs and found a pair of crutches for JD Spent the rest of the morning exploring Angkor Thom, while JD spent it in the shade reading. I am taking a rest now from climbing Phimeanakas, a terraced pyramid, reminiscent of those in the Yucatan of Mexico. The steep climb was well worth it but exhausting in this hot, heavy air.

I'm seated on the broken head of a great stone lion that kept vigil here a thousand years ago, around me are scattered massive blocks, carved with buxom dancers who smile from beneath the jungle cover—fairer faces than that of Ozymandias, but their glory and charm claimed by time nonetheless. Well, no time to get poetic—time rather to find JD and, hopefully, a plate of fried rice. Soon we will take our boat back to Phnom Penh. Tomorrow morning I say good-bye to my friend. These have been treasured days for me. JD will take a prop plane back to Ratanakiri, and I will catch my flight to the east.

CENTRAL SAIGON (HO CHI MINH CITY), VIETNAM

Though it is late as I take up my pen, Saigon is not sleeping—and neither am I. The streets outside still hum and honk with motorcycles and milling crowds. I'm staying in a part of Saigon where "backpackers," as they are called by the locals, hang out in hotels and seedy hostels. And so this district especially attracts solicitations. Pesky motorcycle taxi drivers line the street, many of them using their very limited English for offers of dollar rides to places where cheap drugs and prostitutes can be found. As a result, my evening walk was too annoying, and so I have settled back into my room to write of this remarkable Lord's Day.

I went to church this morning dressed like a Vietnamese version of the Lone Ranger. A man named Kwan met me near the park a short walk from the hotel. He provided me with a hat, sunglasses, a mask, and a long-sleeved jersey, to cover my non-Oriental features. This would lessen suspicion when traveling into the neighborhood where his house church meets. Thus wrapped, I got on the back of his motorcycle, and we took off for a half-hour ride across Saigon. There are a million motorcycles in this city, and with the swirl of dust and exhaust, masks are common; so it's a good way to travel incognito in broad daylight! The streets flow with rivers of motorcycles. At various intervals, the rivers collide—something back home known as an intersection. Here it is a fast game of inches played out in a whirl of wheels, dust, and tangled drivers. And it's fun too!

Kwan took me through an outer district of the city to a house with an open door, which we drove right through. I climbed a back staircase to an upper room where forty people had gathered for worship!

Going to church

This house has been raided by the police on many occasions, but the family that owns it is strong in the Lord. They gave themselves and their house to Christ long ago, and so it is in his hands. At the end of each service during which no one shows up with clubs or handcuffs to break up the service, Kwan explained, the congregation has a time of thanksgiving. And so it was today. God protected this little flock from the wolves—we worshipped in peace.

Afterward I donned my disguise, and Kwan and I slipped back into the swirling streets of Saigon. Later I met up with other house church leaders, and tonight we attended a downtown church. There must have been two hundred in attendance, with many young people.

The streets are quieting down, and night is settling in for a few hours. Since I was young, Saigon has always been a tragic place to me. It was the place where the guys I knew who were just a few years older than me went off to war. Some didn't come back. I remember when all our troops came home and President Nixon asked all Americans at a given time to turn their lights on as a sign to welcome our troops home and as a vigil for those who had fallen in the fight. I watched as porch lights came on all over the neighborhood, and we turned on all the lamps we could. Daddy even turned on the headlights of our car. I will never forget how all those little lights brightened the night. Even though that January evening was long, long ago, I still remember the warmth and joy I felt as the lights came on up and down the streets, and each of us gave something to the celebration. As I look now over the darkening streets of Saigon and think of the Christians I huddled in worship with today, I remember back to that night long ago and how every light made a difference.

SINGAPORE

No matter how often I come here, I'm always amazed to see the power of the gospel at work and am challenged to a faith and vision that matches the scope of the kingdom.

Went to the Chinese construction workers' service held by Gospel Light Christian Church, pastored by my friend Paul Choo. This outreach is one of many to the different people groups who come to Singapore in search of work—Tagalog street evangelism, services for Filipino domestic workers, Bahasa service for Indonesians, Telugu service for mostly Muslim Indian dockworkers, and the construction workers from mainland China. The Chinese are the cheap, unskilled labor force providing a lot of the muscle behind Singapore's big construction projects, such as the new casino and condos. Four hundred men filled the hall tonight, and sixteen came forward at the end to publicly acknowledge their faith in Christ! Last week eight believed. Every week men are saved here! Some come straight from their work sites—their hair caked in dust and their clothes crusty with old sweat. After the service, supper is served—an enormous amount of rice for hundreds of hungry men. Faithfully, week after week, church members spend their Sunday afternoons and evenings cooking and serving. These acts of love are the opening illustrations of the gospel message before the pastor ever steps behind the pulpit. While some of the men are getting their dinner, others are getting their hair cut. Since a haircut can cost these men nearly a day's wage, they welcome this ministry from the church members—even if the cut isn't the latest style, and the barbers are learning on them. Tonight, even I was recruited to cut and got a quick lesson. But it's really easy—put the trimmer on the number four setting and follow the contours of the head!

Afterward we went over to the Telugu service in another part of the city. This is the outreach to the dockworkers from India—mostly Muslims from Hyderabad—who, like the Chinese, come here for work. Jacob, a Telugu Indian, leads the work. He is a computer tech here in Singapore. IT is how he makes a living; sharing Christ is how he lives. The only thing he needed was a place to meet. One church after another turned him away. Since the men were coming at night after a long shift at the dockyard, Jacob needed to feed them, but some pastors felt that the Indian food would leave the smell of curry in the church, and so they all said no. Unfortunately, these Christians see church as a building and not as people for whom Christ died. The Gospel Light group took the Indians in, and the work has more than doubled since I first met Jacob three years ago. Every other month they baptize twenty or so men—men with names like Mohammed and Osama!

Not all the gospel stories have happy endings. Ika, a Muslim woman from Java, came to Singapore for work as a domestic. Ika heard the gospel here and believed in Jesus. She loved to be with God's people on the Lord's Day, growing in her faith. She wanted to be in church every Sunday, but her employer only permitted her two Sundays off a month. Another man offered to hire Ika and give her every Sunday off—only at one-third less pay. She took the job—two extra Sundays in church a month! But the man cheated her—he gave her no days off, and then fired her. She returned to her family in Java with little to show for her time in Singapore except her faith. Ika's husband opened her suitcase at the bus station and found her Bible. He refused to allow her to come back home—even to see their son. The last that was heard from her, she was wandering and looking for work. She had called back to the church to ask them to mail her baptismal certificate. She wanted it as a token of her testimony and of her time with the people she loved to be with. Tonight I think of my sister Ika—poor, rejected, wandering, like those in Hebrews 11, "destitute, afflicted, mistreated—of whom the world was not worthy" (11:37–38).

ILOILO, CENTRAL PHILIPPINES

A typhoon delayed my flights from Singapore to Manila and then to Iloilo. Despite the high winds and driving rain, the plane took off into the dark sky. I prayed to the One who can speak, "Peace, be still!" to the storm. Other than hitting a few "washboards" on the way and getting kicked sideways once, we bounced into the Iloilo airport last night in good shape.

This morning as I write, the sky is clearing. Beyond the coconut palms, the blue mountains of Iloilo rise above the swirling mist. It is my birthday, and it is Mother's Day. It has been a year since Mama was taken from our arms into the arms of the Lord. The grief and separation are still fresh. She would not be surprised to find me here today—on a little island far away in the South Pacific. We were always close, though often I was far away. I guess it's still that way.

Tomorrow I take a boat to the tiny island of Guimaras, where pastors from all over the archipelago will gather. Dozens of passengers died yesterday when the typhoon swamped several boats. I pray the Lord will keep all our people safe as we cross these treacherous waters.

CAMP NIKOS, GUIMARAS ISLAND, PHILIPPINES

The soldiers are returning from the front. Pastors and their wives, colporteurs, and campus workers are coming here for a few days of R & R. Traveling by bumboat, by jeepney, by motorcycle, and even on foot, they come from islands all across the Philippines, from southeast Asia, and even from China. This is a brief respite behind the lines before launching the summer evangelistic campaigns and other ministries. Many of them are "barefoot pastors"—the poor pastors laboring in remote, rural areas among the last and the least. Most of them are weary, and some are wounded; so the fellowship with each other and around the Word is especially sweet. Some of them have to contend with Communist guerillas, like the New People's Army south of here on Mindanao, as well as the murderous Abu Sayyef and other Muslim terrorists. These barefoot pastors also face the routine challenges of walking deep into the jungle or crossing swollen rivers to take the gospel to scattered villages. Yet for these soldiers returning from the front lines, this is not a field hospital. They are not showing their scars but sharing their victories and praising God that they are counted worthy to suffer for him.

The preaching is fervent, and so are the temperatures. I am struggling to untangle the Tagalog from the broken English of the man who is preaching now. Hand fans flutter across the gathering, and a few electric fans stir the thick air. Even the pages of my journal are limp with dampness. The cisterns ran dry this morning, so water had to be pumped from the river. My hot water for coffee started out coffee-colored. But a hard rain is now beginning to sweep the camp, washing over the coconut grove and beating on the roof with deafening effect. The cisterns will soon be filled and coffee made from rainwater will be flowing again!

BAHAS ISLAND, NEAR THE SULU SEA

After the morning services, several of us took a bumboat out to this little island, which seems to be inhabited mostly by hermit crabs, which shuffle along the shore and wade among old coconuts that bob in the tide. These afternoons are to me among the most precious times of the camp—talking about what the Lord is doing and the stories of grace and the gospel on the front lines. These people remind me that "God chose what is foolish in the world . . . what is weak . . . what is low and despised . . . to bring to nothing things that are" (1 Cor. 1:27–28).

Welma and her mother Milagros are two who wouldn't count for much in the world's eyes—maybe not much even in the professional Christian world either. They are ordinary people doing extraordinary things by the power of God. Welma was a Filipino domestic worker in Singapore—a single mom with little education and little future. Through a gospel tract, she read John 3:16. She told me that the word "whoever" stuck in her mind when she realized that even a poor migrant house servant like herself was included in that worldwide word. By faith, she believed on the Son.

Now Welma shares the gospel wherever people are gathered back on her island of Panay in the central Philippines—women, children, dock workers, prisoners, farmers in the field, even the aboriginal Negritos (a small, dark people who live deep in the jungles of Panay). In the past two years, Welma's witness has been instrumental in starting twenty-three house churches! They don't gather a congregation and then launch a building program before starting the next church. Brick and mortar would slow down the brush fire. The churches meet in backyards or under mango trees. The barefoot pastors are stretched to keep up with the pace, holding worship services on different days of the week.

The story of Welma's mother Milagros is another great chapter in the advance of the gospel in Panay. When Welma returned from Singapore two years ago, Milagros immediately noticed a difference in her daughter and asked her why she had changed so much. Welma told her about John 3:16—the incredible love of God that "whoever" trusted Christ for salvation would have everlasting life! And Milagros believed.

Early the next morning—it was just five o'clock—Welma was awakened by her mother saying, "Get up. Come quickly. There are people here to see you." Welma stirred from her sleep and said, "No," thinking the neighbors were there to borrow money, since she had just returned from working in Singapore. But Milagros insisted that she get dressed and come quickly. Welma got up and walked out of their little house, and there seven of her mom's friends stood waiting. "Now," Milagros said to her daughter, "tell them what you told me last night!"

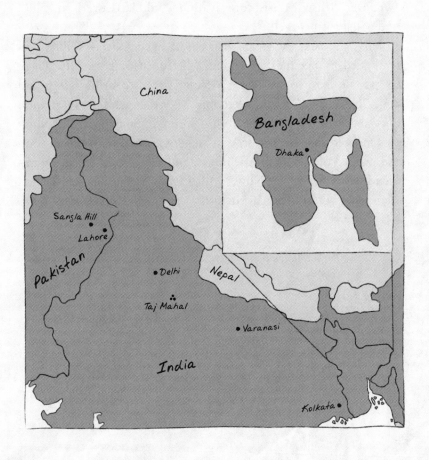

China

Bangladesh

Dhaka

Sangla Hill

Lahore

Pakistan

Delhi

Nepal

Taj Mahal

Varanasi

India

Kolkata

5

SOULS OF THE BRAVE

Bangladesh, India, and Pakistan

Sea Angel

"For we do not want you to be unaware, brothers, of the affliction we experienced in Asia. For we were so utterly burdened beyond our strength that we despaired of life itself. Indeed, we felt that we had received the sentence of death" (2 Cor. 1:8–9).

These are strong words. Affliction. Utterly burdened. Beyond strength. Despair. Sentence of death. Ironically, while Paul did not want the Corinthians to be ignorant of the ultimate trial he faced, he never actually fills in the details of what brought him to the doorway of death. Someday I'll ask him. But in the meantime, I think the blanks have been left for Christ's followers in every age and every danger to fill in. When we come to the end of strength, of options, of answers, perhaps even of life, then the Lord lets us see not our death, but his; not our fragile life, but his endless one—and ours, too. Paul said that the danger and despair he and his friends endured served to "make us rely not on ourselves but on God who raises the dead. . . . On him we have set our hope" (2 Cor. 1:9b–10).

Paul's first-century Asia is our modern-day Turkey, but in the twenty-first century, across a wider swath of Asia, I have met brothers and sisters whose lives are poured out in risk-taking, gospel ministry. Yet in pouring out their lives, they have experienced the living Christ in them and through them and for them. Here are their stories.

DHAKA, BANGLADESH

Reached Dhaka late yesterday after two days and two nights of travel. Caught a little sleep with what was left of the night, and then set out this morning in a rickshaw in search of a good cup of coffee and a rendezvous with a friend. Bicycle rickshaws are cheap and plentiful. The drivers are called *wallahs*, and they all seem to be scrawny and tough as gristle. They are usually dressed in a *lungi*—a simple, printed cotton, wrap-around skirt, a staple of men's fashion here. It is estimated that there are four hundred thousand rickshaw wallahs in Dhaka alone—a workforce greater in size than many cities of the world. In Dhaka though, with its population of over twelve million, rickshaw wallahs are just another part of its crowded street life.

Reached the coffee shop, which was already aswirl with customers and fine brew. Double-barrel shots were flowing from a stainless steel espresso machine, and milk and steam were teaming up to top off cappuccinos. Met up with Ryan. He and his family have labored in the gospel here for more than ten years. A native Alabaman, he looks like he could have been a wide receiver for the Crimson Tide. Ryan had many career path options when he graduated from college, but he chose above all else to be a fisher of men. Ryan and his family are engaged in community development projects in the delta region, an area known as the Mouths of the Ganges. His project work gives him access and opportunities to share Christ and disciple believers in a difficult part of this difficult country. The number of Christians is growing in this Muslim stronghold and so, too, is the persecution. Tomorrow I will go with Ryan down into the Mouths, so that I can meet some of my new brothers.

Early afternoon. Caught the closing spectacle of Durga Puja. Bangladesh is 90 percent Muslim and nearly 10 percent Hindu, leaving little room for the rest, including the quarter of 1 percent of Christians in this country. The festival at Durga Puja is the biggest event on the Hindu calendar year. Temporary temples, called *pandals*, are raised in every Hindu community. The one nearby was impressive, built of bamboo and covered with peach and pink silk. The tent housed Durga, a ten-armed goddess, flanked by her pantheon of idols and a frenzy of followers, who were beating drums and shouting for their mute mother-god. Durga's devotees swirled about, marked with blood-red vermillion on their foreheads, believing it a third eye to see the unseen; but it's all blindness—just makeup for a make-believe god in a makeshift temple. Since the festival was almost over, the *pandal* was already being taken down— and Durga was about to be taken away to be paraded to the nearest river and then sunk into the netherworld for another year. The poor, eager for a load of firewood or framing for some shelter, got a jump start hauling home pieces of the tent—at least some good will come of all this.

DHAKA, BANGLADESH

Set out this morning on an MAF flight from Dhaka to the Mouths of the Ganges. Missionary Aviation Fellowship operates one plane for all of Bangladesh, but it's perfectly suited for a land that's half water—it's an amphibious Cessna. It can take off on land, cruise at one hundred and sixty miles per hour, and then turn most any river into a runway. Our pilot, Emil, is a native of Switzerland and a veteran missionary aviator with a cool, can-do attitude. His earliest experience in aviation wasn't flying planes—it was jumping out of them as a paratrooper in the Swiss Air Force! He told me he sensed back then that God was calling him to pursue missionary aviation. That was over twenty-five years ago, and his assignments since read like a catalog of hard places—Chad, Uganda, Sudan, Madagascar, Cambodia, and Bangladesh. Emil's outlook, like any good pilot, is always forward and upward. He was made to fly.

We quickly climbed over the sprawl of Dhaka, and Emil took us just over a mile high, where we had a great panorama of this watery world. Bangladesh is one of the most densely populated countries in the world—half the population of the United States packed onto land the size of Iowa. But the squeeze is, in part, because a third of the country is under water—and during monsoon, that percentage can rise to over half! Bangladesh sits in a disaster zone of geography. At its northern border, Bangladesh is only a hike away from Nepal and the Himalayas—the rooftop of the world. Three major rivers, including the Ganges and the Brahmaputra, cascade down from the Himalayas into this mostly sea level country—it's like a giant drain. And in monsoon season, these rivers and their offspring swell and burst like bad pipes. Then to the south, the Bay of Bengal births cyclones, which slam the country and take an enormous toll. A super cyclone twenty years ago killed 138,000 people and left ten million homeless. A more recent one claimed fifteen thousand lives. In the aftermath of that cyclone, this plane was the only civilian aircraft that could reach into the flooded devastation with supplies and relief teams. Survivors started calling this seaplane the "Sea Angel." Today though, our view is a picture of peace. The sun traces its finger over the thin, green veneer of land laced with lazy rivers the color of cappuccino.

Reached a rough river town about twenty miles south of Khulna. From the air it is more like a ramshackle sprawl of rusty roofs, huddled along the muddy channel. Emil circled to find an open spot away from fishing boats, and then glided down to the water, lightly skiing on it. Then, suddenly, the "bird" became a "fish," and we were a boat, floating with the rest of the boats. Emil made it all look so easy, as if he had done this a few hundred times before!

A welcoming committee of kids came out to greet us—some curious, some mischievous. Emil had arranged for a boat to take Ryan and me to shore, where we docked and went on to meet eight believers—men with names like Mohammed and Abdul, who have come to Christ out of Islam. Ryan has been discipling them as they follow Christ in the fellowship of his sufferings. After coffee and introductions, Ryan opened the Word, followed by a time of prayer and hymns. I particularly enjoyed the singing. One of the men named Jahru served as the cantor, calling the tunes as the other men joined in. In Bengali they sang "Jesus's name is wonderful . . . we are worshipping in the name of Jesus!" Christ, whose name is above every name, is the One that these men have left all to follow. In many cases, their families treat them as if they are already dead—and wish it were so. Yet, even though they are despised and rejected by men, they have joy and grace and courage enough to speak of their Savior. There are now about two hundred believers in this region who have come to Christ out of Islam. They are scattered in little house churches, as the good news spreads by word of mouth. Even in our little gathering today, there were three generations of Christians—Jahru led Jamal to Christ, and then Jamal led Hasan to faith and to the fellowship of Christ's sufferings.

Afterward Ryan and I sat beneath a mango tree with these three men to hear their stories. Hasan has taken refuge here, because if he returns home, he will be killed. While sharing Christ in a house meeting last year, he was betrayed and then dragged out into the town and beaten, slapped with sandals, and publicly humiliated by a crowd calling for his death. The two other men have suffered similarly in their homes and villages. As Jahru said, "Each believer has his own story, but all must walk through the fire." I hardly knew what to say to my brothers, so we prayed—and continue to pray—"Lord Jesus, these three men are going through the fire. Help them to know that you are the fourth Man in the fire with them. Be their shield and companion. May even those who have caused this fire fall down in fear and faith and declare that you alone are God!"

Late afternoon we walked to the docks, where Ryan arranged for a boat to take us out in the channel to rendezvous with the seaplane. We flew here today, but normally Ryan takes his motorcycle onboard a riverboat as far as this port, and then goes deep into the delta to disciple struggling, suffering Christians—hard, backwater work.

Dusk was settling over this raw river town. Bells, boat horns, and coughing diesel engines mixed with the call to prayer from a chorus of mosques. We were in the river for only a short time before the seaplane swept in. It was as if we had a front-row seat at an airshow, as Emil landed with a splash and a spray of golden light.

As our plane lifted off and leveled out, a red sun sat smoldering in the west. I thought of my suffering brothers left behind, and of Jahru's words, "All must walk through the fire." Below us, rivers ran like tears down the face of the country, and a certain sadness haunted me as we reached dark Dhaka.

DAY OF SACRIFICE, DHAKA, BANGLADESH

The mosques echoed with morning prayers, as men bent to the task of sharpening knives for the sacrifice. Cows were tied up along the street. Calm, quiet to their fate, some settled on the pavement as if they were still in their familiar pasture rather than in this hard city with its strange noises—the clamor of the streets, the grinding of long blades. Here in Bangladesh—and all across the Muslim world today—cows, goats, and sheep are being slain as an act of "righteousness." Within two hours, tens of thousands of cows in this city alone will be killed, turning Dhaka into one great slaughterhouse.

This Muslim holy day is called *Eid al Qurbani*. *Qurbani* means "sacrifice" and recalls the time when God commanded Abraham to sacrifice his son Ishmael. Both father and son, in acts of supreme obedience—one to kill and one to be killed—went to the very edge of the act. But before the blade fell on the throat of the son-sacrifice,

God stayed Abraham's hand and provided a ram as a substitute for Ishmael. Of course, the whole story is a half-fiction, a reworking of the Genesis account centuries after the fact so that Ishmael, the Arabs' ancestor, is the hero and Isaac is written out.

When the prayers were done, men set about their bloody work. Each animal was bound, forced down, and its head turned toward Mecca. An imam, carrying a long, curved knife, acted as the priest, taking the scimitar to the jugular. The imam went quickly from one animal to another, leaving them with gaping throats and a sickening struggle. Blood flowed in the streets—fresh, red, brilliant blood.

Day of Sacrifice

For each animal, the head of the family presented the imam with a list of names of those to be atoned for by that sacrifice—and who, no doubt, would also share in the beef afterward. Both those on the list and those who laid their hands on the offering would be atoned for by this shedding of blood. There was some faint shadow here, some husk of truth—like a Christless Old Testament, only more blood and more death—but no life.

As I walked among them, some of the men were eager to explain to me what this sacrifice was all about. They rehearsed how Abraham was about to sacrifice Ishmael, but God provided a substitute. An animal died so that an obedient man could live. All of them spoke of the need for a substitute—at least they knew *that* much of the truth. But what they don't know—yet—is that God did not just provide a substitute; God *was* the substitute—and not for the obedient, but for the disobedient—for sinners like me, and like the men here with blood on their hands. Unlike the *Qurbani*, which year after year claims a million or more animals, this Sacrifice was of such force that it was offered *once*—and *for all*. So complete was it, that with a loud voice Jesus could cry, "It is finished!" But finished at such cost! The crucifixion was no poignant painting in a gilded frame. It was red and real. It was blood-sodden ground and sickening agony. It was cruel indifference. It was bleeding to death—alone.

As I struggled through the blind crowd and passed the carcasses they had made, I glimpsed the horror and the wonder of Calvary. Thoughts of the cross overwhelmed me with sorrow and joy over Jesus, my willing substitute. There's no vocabulary to match such grace. It's "love beyond degree," as the hymn says.

> My God, why would You shed Your blood—
> So pure and undefiled—
> To make a sinful one like me
> Your chosen, precious child?[1]

KOLKATA, INDIA

Flew to Kolkata to meet up with my friend Aashish. His gospel ministry over the years has been marked by compassion, courage, and grace under fire. He and I are going to travel by train across the length of northern India. Since reading Paul Theroux's *The Great Railway Bazaar*, I have wanted to see India this way. Railroads are to India what the interstate is to America, but unlike our highways, it's more than just a way to "get there." It's a way of life, too. At least that is what I imagine and hope to find out over the next few weeks.

But I want to see more than the country and its people. I want to see their gods—for India is a land of gods. Some Hindu scholars estimate there are over three hundred million of them. There are so many, in fact, that the temples cannot contain them. They spill out into the streets and creep into corners and crevices and deep into hearts as well, for India is a land of idolaters.

There seems to be a disconnect between this India and the one that's taking its place in the twenty-first century as the world's service center. Its talented people are making significant contributions to technology and medicine, and with a billion plus people, India is a force on the international stage. Yet many of these same educated Hindus will cut their hair and offer it to their family god in an act of devotion or worship cow dung. Apart from the chain-breaking power of the gospel, the Hindus' thinking cannot help but be dominated by the gods they have made, for their gods are the sum of all their fears and all their fantasies. On the dark side of high-rise India, Hindu hate grows against Christians. It's a hatred that shows itself in daily discrimination—and occasionally spills over into acts of violence. Tensions still run high in the neighboring state of Orissa, where scores of Christians were killed, hundreds of homes and churches burned, and fifty thousand displaced. Many still live in squalid refugee camps, afraid to return to face death threats from their Hindu neighbors.

Kolkata is the chief city of the Bengali people—with Dhaka running a close second. But whereas Dhaka on the Bangladesh side is marked with mosques, on the India side, Kolkata is filled with idols. Islam and Hinduism divide the Bengali people as much as national boundaries do.

The two principal goddesses here in Kolkata are Kali and Durga. Went to the temple of Kali this afternoon. Aashish and I had to remove our shoes and have water from the Ganges squirted on our hands, but when the temple priest tried to mark my forehead, I gave him the evil eye. Went into this temple of doom which celebrates Kali, the goddess of death. Her image decorates the stalls and billboards around her temple. She has a blood-red tongue that hangs down to her waist and a necklace of severed heads, and, like most Hindu gods, she seems to have a few too many arms. She looks like something from a bad movie. But this is no joke to those who come to worship her, praying and paying for protection from sudden death. Two men stood near me. They were waiting in earnest as the priest marked their foreheads with a tika, which smudged in the sweat of their haunted faces. I thought of the verse in Hebrews, "Through fear of death were subject to lifelong slavery" (Heb. 2:15). What a miserable place this is. The air is thick with smoke, fear, and evil—like opening a furnace door to hell.

ON THE RAIL, KOLKATA TO VARANASI

Set out for Serampore at first light. Two hundred years ago this was home to the intrepid missionary William Carey and his team. Carey, the "father of modern missions," had a vision for worldwide evangelization when few others had a big enough view of God to see it. Carey's example of vision, action, and endurance has meant much to me personally. I can hardly believe I'm here, walking through what were only pages in a book before. On the banks of the Hooghly River, I found the cross which marks the spot where, after six long years of persistent ministry, Carey baptized the first Indian convert. Nearby are the college that he started and a little museum that holds a few brittle copies of the Bibles he translated. A mile or so away we found the cemetery where he, his family, and his colleagues are buried. Aashish coaxed the caretaker's daughter to open the gate for us. In the corner of the cemetery, Carey's grave is marked, as he directed, by a simple stone and epitaph—"A wretched, poor, and helpless worm, on Thy kind arms I fall."

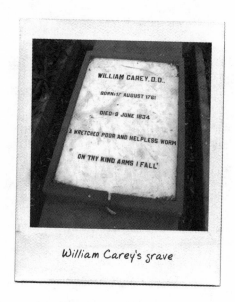

William Carey's grave

Sadly, most Indians today have never heard of William Carey or his God. Serampore, like every other Indian town, is stuffed with idols. A century after Carey's death, his college had departed from the faith, embracing liberalism, shunning the message of the gospel that Carey had so faithfully preached. Today it has become just a nice place to go to college. Most of the faculty and students are non-Christians. I am left feeling that there should be more to show for such a life; but Carey's monuments aren't made of bricks or marble, but rather something so much bigger. He gave India the Bible. In fact, he gave this polyglot people with its tangle of tongues several Bibles. He translated the entire Bible into six major Indian languages and portions of the Bible into twenty-nine other Asian languages. Carey knew that "the entrance of thy words giveth light" (Ps. 119:130 KJV). In the lineage of Luther and Tyndale, he believed that the very best preacher was the Bible in the language of the people. Across India, from Afghanistan to Burma, people can now read and receive the good news in their heart language. *This* is Carey's living legacy.

Making gods

Afterward returned to Kolkata. Before heading to the train station, stopped at Kumartuli, a tangle of alleys where the idol-makers ply their trade. They twist some straw, shape some mud over it, add some paint and sparkles, and voila! "Behold your god!" Just as they were in Bangladesh, the Bengalis here are in the midst of the festival of Durga Puja. Durga's ten arms make her look like Spider-Woman to me. I thought of the words of Jeremiah, "Their idols are like scarecrows in a cucumber field, and they cannot speak; they have to be carried, for they cannot walk. Do not be afraid of them, for they cannot do evil, neither is it in them to do good. . . . There is no breath in them. They are worthless, a work of delusion" (Jer. 10:5, 14–15). The blindness of these people is profound; like their gods, they are born without eyes.

Took the 8:30 train this evening. The rail station in Kolkata is a microcosm of India. The sights, smells, and crowds are all here. The stench of urine and incense hangs in the air over a platform smeared with spit and excrement. Beggars, dogs, the deranged, all mingle with the chaotic crowds that, like me, rushed to find their train. We've settled in for the night with fifteen hours ahead of us.

VARANASI, INDIA

I woke to a vast green sea of rice as our train lurched on toward Varanasi. I made coffee in my water bottle in search of consciousness. Had a night of only napping, accompanied by a chorus of snorers that sounded like a company of organs—no, worse—bagpipes! The train is much quieter now that it's morning. Travelers are lolling about, bored and sleepy, as our train sails through the emerald sea of rice on the plains of Uttar Pradesh.

My train window is a kaleidoscope of life along the rail—there's a man living under an umbrella, his possessions all under its shadow; a one-armed man rushing to catch the train, his sleeve sweeping past him; giggling schoolgirls tripping along a dusty road. In the distant rice fields women in bright saris bend to their tasks, dotting the green void like a string of gems.

Reached Varanasi. Our hired driver here is a man named Somnat. He has been a big help in getting around the city. He is a devotee of Ganesh, the elephant-headed god. Aashish took the opportunity to share Christ—*Ishu Masih*—with him. Aashish's approach is to ask searching questions, modeled after Jesus's approach to engaging in gospel conversations. May the Lord give Somnat light to know him.

For much of its three thousand years, Varanasi was called Kashi, "city of light." I think nothing could be further from the truth. This is the holiest city of Hinduism, their mecca huddled along the muddy Ganges, which they worship as a goddess and believe that its waters can wash away sins.

Walked toward the river and the ghats, the steps that descend into it. The streets were filled with holy cows and holy men. The sheer scale of this spectacle gives weight to the worship. When you get past the hucksters and the backpackers here to smoke cheap hash, when you get past the boatmen and the souvenir sellers, there are millions who come here each year to drink this sacred water and to wash away their sins. Those who sit hopelessly scrubbing at their sins in a muddy river do not yet know of grace, of the Lord's awesome work spoken of in Ezekiel: "I will sprinkle clean water on you, and you shall be clean from all your uncleannesses, and from all your idols I will cleanse you. And I will give you a new heart, and a new spirit I will put within you" (36:25–26).

Negotiated with a boatman to take us out on the Ganges for a few bucks. The Ganges was swirling and swollen, overflowing from the heavy monsoon rains upstream, but it was good to get away from the stench of the shore and get out on the open waters in the gathering dusk. I wanted to see the ghat known as Manikarnika, the place of the burning of the dead. Here fires burn continuously, consuming up to a hundred corpses a day. Boats tethered to the shore were piled high with the wood which fuels the eternal flame. The people believe that to die here and to have their ashes scattered on the Ganges leads to instant nirvana, freeing them from the otherwise endless cycle of birth and rebirth. This is the portal to paradise. Immortality, though, comes with a price. The wood has to be bought—and for the lowest caste, their dead are often burned en masse. If they can't afford enough wood, the half-burned corpses are simply dumped into the river. Over a century ago, Mark Twain took a boat on the Ganges to this very point and wrote with purposeful sarcasm of Manikarnika:

> The fire used is sacred, of course—for there is money in it. Ordinary fire is forbidden; there is no money in it. I was told that this sacred fire is all furnished by one person, and that he has a monopoly of it and charges a good price for it. To get to paradise from India is an expensive thing. Every detail connected with the matter costs something, and helps to fatten a priest.[2]

The bodies of men are covered in white shrouds and women in orange, and we saw two dead women being readied for the funeral pyre. Above their corpses, flames burned bright with flesh. We moved on as the oarsmen pulled against the current. Last light brightened the river, but evil hung in the air along with the stench of death as night descended over the Ganges.

DELHI, INDIA

Reached the Indian capital last night in a downpour, and went out this morning to see some of the temples of Delhi. At the temples, people lined up in the rain to get some "karma credit." One grand temple, like a marble mausoleum, was filled with gods: the Rat god, the Monkey god, the voluptuous Parvati, Krishna, the blue-skinned avatar of Vishnu, and every other manifestation of people's creative genius for manufacturing make-believe gods—gods of power and fear, gods of sex and luck and greed. Their worshippers are walking dead. I recognize them, for in my own way I have walked among them—and would be there still apart from the living Christ!

The Birla temple was built for the high-caste Brahmans, priests of prejudice. Their symbol is the swastika. Of course, many ancient cultures used the swastika motif, but it's interesting that Hitler borrowed—not invented—the swastika as a mark of Aryan arrogance. In the whole wide world, the symbol is now condemned, except among three groups: skinheads, Muslim extremists (who admire Hitler's ability to murder so many Jews), and high-caste Hindus. The Birla temple was covered with swastikas and reminded me of pictures of Nazi rallies in the 1930s, but this has nothing to do with Germany. It has everything to do with India. The Brahmans stamp the swastika on their shops, homes—even their company trucks.

The caste system is deep in the DNA of the Indian people—it is a system built on pride and prejudice that predates memory. At the bottom of this social ladder are the low caste, the Dalits, the Untouchables—one hundred and sixty million of them. For them, from the moment of birth, life is itself an unpardonable sin. Even though race-based slavery was abolished in most of the world long ago, in India it is made into a religious rite. The Dalits are given the lowest places, and the country is built on their back-breaking labor. They live in apartments fit for no one else or in garbage dumps, which are the Untouchables' subdivision. And so the Unclean do their work, embracing their burdensome karma of poverty, heavy toil, and exclusion. When Mark Twain traveled through India long ago, he wrote, Indians are "a curious people. With them, all life seems to be sacred except human life."[3]

TAJ MAHAL

The clouds have lifted, and the rain has stopped for now. Took a four-hour drive from Delhi to Agra to see the Taj Mahal, India's wonder of the world. We are traveling along what was the famous Grand Trunk Road back in the days when England's empire covered the subcontinent. I can picture British regiments, artillery, and horse-soldiers stirring up clouds of dust on their march to Kabul or Lucknow. Today dust and diesel fumes swirl instead, as truck traffic jockeys for position on a road that Rudyard Kipling might still recognize. Truck stops have replaced the old camel caravansaries, but travelers' needs are still the same—a little rest and refreshment before returning to the road to Agra. Along that crowded, chaotic road, we had some close encounters that nearly turned holy cow into holy hamburger!

Reached Agra late morning and bargained for a horse-drawn rickshaw to take us the last mile to India's crown jewel. Aashish assumed the role of tour guide with gusto. As he led me to the Taj Mahal, he insisted that I not look until the magic moment when all was in view, or as he put it, "Like finally seeing a bride on her wedding day!" So I shuffled along behind him, staring at my feet, until Aashish said, "Now!" And there was the Taj Mahal in all its stunning, shimmering symmetry. It's no wonder it's a wonder of the world! Aashish is right. Everyone knows what the Taj Mahal looks like—it's one of the most recognized places in the world—but actually seeing it in all its rich detail is like the difference between a feast and reading the menu. Built by Shah Jahan when Muslims ruled India four hundred years ago, the Taj Mahal is the tomb for his favorite wife. It has been called a monument of love. But it's just as much a monument of cruelty, for the shah rewarded the builders by having their hands chopped off, so they could not repeat their work of wonder. And at the end of all its magnificence, it's just a tomb.

Afterward set out for Delhi again. At four o'clock, Aashish needed his afternoon tea, and we all needed a stretch. The driver took us into oncoming traffic, for here the rules of the road follow the book of Judges, where "everyone did what was right in his own eyes" (17:6). Dodged head-on collisions and reached the Maharaja, a truck stop and trinket shop, without incident. Enjoyed masala tea, a smooth spicy brew of ginger, cardamom, and cloves with tea and milk. It's like liquid pumpkin pie. It was good to share this day and be refreshed with laughter and good tea before returning to the road. Still two hours to Delhi.

DELHI TO WESTERN INDIA
Another night train.

We set out for the west. The Lord has led us and kept us all along the way. As the psalmist said, "You hem me in, behind and before" (Ps. 139:5). I just heard that terrorists blew up the rail line we took out of Kolkata a few days ago, cutting off train traffic between Kolkata and Varanasi. About the same time, several leading Communists were assassinated in Kolkata. Now the whole city is under police curfew; so if we were still in Kolkata, we'd be there for a while.

I'm relieved to be on the move, but I'm not the only one—Aashish is going home, after being away for several weeks. Aashish carries many burdens and battle scars. His gospel ministry has been marked by patient plowing and planting and waiting for harvest from hard ground. Tonight, though, he's just eager to see his family again.

SOMEWHERE IN WESTERN INDIA
Reached Aashish's home this morning. A day to catch up and clean up. This is his refuge, and today, it's mine, too. His wife, Sujayah, prepared a fine breakfast for us. Sujayah is Aashish's perfect partner. Their ministry together has been a battle from the start. She

is a woman with a heart as big as the gospel, and she's as brave as Caesar.

Sujayah graciously offered to do my laundry while Aashish and I went to run errands. We took an auto rickshaw downtown, squeezing into the back of it, and then further squeezing into the tightly packed traffic. Most of the time, the rickshaws were so close we could have joined arms, formed a chorus line, and danced to the tune of a hundred horns. I've seen a lot of the world, but for sheer, death-defying entertainment, there's nothing like Indian roads, swirling with cars and cows—and even camels clopping through the madness.

We found a money changer and exchanged dollars for rupees. Then Aashish decided he needed a haircut. We found one barber operating under a tree. He only charged thirty cents, but factoring in the possible hidden medical costs of a scalp disease, we opted for a three-dollar haircut at a Walmart wannabe, an Indian chain called Big Bazaar.

Returned by late afternoon. I think Aashish has some British blood in him, for by four o'clock it's always "tea time." Sujayah stirred up some of her famous tea for us, mixing and frothing it with an experienced hand.

Later enjoyed supper with the whole family, and after we ate, they included me in their family devotions. I loved hearing them sing, especially one Hindi song about *Ishu Masih*. Translated, it says, "Jesus Christ is my song, He's my music. And I will sing always about Him because He is the sweetest song." On their wall is an embroidered prayer, "God bless our home." He has, indeed, blessed this home. The love, the light, and the music of Jesus here were in sharp, life-and-death contrast to the scene in the streets below their apartment window, where the ten-day festival of Ganesh—the elephant-headed god—was under way. Worshippers were beating drums and shouting to be heard by their deaf god. The priest put the mark of this beast on all who came, as revelers danced in the darkness.

146

SOMEWHERE IN WESTERN INDIA

Traveled today to a little beachhead of gospel work in hostile Hindu territory. A key part of Aashish's ministry is mentoring men—faithful men who will be able to teach others also. Aashish has a *gurukul* system of teaching, which simply means that when the teacher calls, the students come and they spend the day together. Though Aashish has a PhD and is a gifted teacher, Aashish's "school" would be considered a failure by Western standards because it has not produced a single graduate. No one ever graduates from this school. Many of these pastors have been with him for a decade. There are no gowns or mortarboards, no diplomas. Aashish's approach is to teach, mentor, and build leaders equipped to stand and proclaim the gospel, even in the face of persecution. Aashish often reminds these men that "pastor" is not a title; it's a responsibility. Aashish does not pay salaries to these pastors. He has told them, "All I promise you is if I have one piece of bread, I will give you half." They are partially supported by their small churches, and they supplement their tables by farming. Some Western mission organizations have tried to "buy" them with bigger salaries and offers of buildings. These are organizations that grow by acquisition, rather than by gospel addition. Aashish tells his men, "Focus on making God big. If you do, everything else will fall into its place. But if you focus on making yourself big, everything will fall apart." These men have been forged in the hard advance of the kingdom of Christ in this part of India. They are a band of brothers, and there was special joy today because this was their first time back together after many weeks apart. Aashish told me afterward, "We are addicted to each other."

Early evening, we took a road into the hinterlands, driving through lush stretches of corn and sweet cane and over rivers flowing full with monsoon waters. All along the way, Ganesh worshippers were reveling—some were parading in the road, tying up traffic; others were kneeling along a riverbank, chanting and playing with fire. In one town, the little plastic elephant idol looked vacantly at his subjects, who danced to drums and tossed purple and pink powder into the air.

Visited Pastor Ramesh and his wife Sevanthi. Enjoyed my time with this dear couple and their daughters. Aashish says Ramesh is like John the Baptist, a man who can "go before." That is, he's a good pathfinder, being the first to take the gospel into villages. Aashish, Ramesh, and the other pastors have a goal of reaching fifteen new villages each year, and over the past decade they have reached over one hundred and seventy villages.

Ramesh and Sevanthi are gracious people. Their home is typical for the villages in this region. The walls are made of split bamboo, woven together like a basket and then covered inside and out with a mud and manure stucco. Besides being a good binder, the manure actually serves as a pesticide to protect the bamboo. The dirt floor was well kept, and the kitchen was well organized. Recently Sujayah helped Sevanthi get a small gas stove. Before, Sevanthi had to burn wood or dung, which consumed lots of time to gather, and the smoke was hard on her lungs. She put the stove to good use tonight as she prepared us delicious tea made with buffalo milk.

Sevanthi is illiterate, yet she is memorizing Scripture. In fact, half the Christians in these rural areas can't read or write, but Aashish tells them, "Don't feel sorry for yourselves. Use what you have. You know what a ten Rupee note is versus a fifty Rupee note because someone told you. It's the same in spiritual things. Learn from others." Sevanthi's children have taught her to memorize Scripture, and this year she has memorized Ephesians 2.

The sun was drawing down across the plains of Hindustan when we parted ways. Being with Ramesh and Sevanthi was a sweet conclusion to this day. I see the fruit of Aashish and Sujayah's mentoring in them, but even more, I see the fruit of the Spirit in them. I felt a little sad about saying good-bye—even though we had never met before today, we're family.

SOMEWHERE IN WESTERN INDIA

Drove out for an evangelistic meeting. The sky was threatening, and black clouds brewed a downpour, spiked with lightning. Aashish and I reached the church before sunset—and just before the sky broke. Some people rode in the back of tractors to reach the church, but most walked. This village is unusual because the believers here have a church building. In many places, locals won't allow property to be sold to believers or church buildings to be raised. But here, the village chief became a Christian, and he gave a portion of his rice field for the church. So who could object?

As is their custom, the men and women sat separately on the floor, and their music filled the place. Aashish preached in Hindi, and Ramesh interpreted the message into the dominant tribal language of Gamit. Aashish preached from Acts 17 about "Jesus among the Idols," recalling when the apostle Paul in Athens, amid the clutter of idols, made known to the Greeks their "unknown god" and preached Christ to them. Many Hindus look at Jesus as just another god, just another idol. Hindu priests have told Aashish, "We don't mind you preaching about Jesus. You just can't say that he is the only way of salvation." Aashish replies, "Then I have nothing to preach!"

In this part of India, one of the most hostile to the gospel, Christians are outnumbered a thousand to one. And so, under the dominance of numbers, the force of discriminatory laws, the threat of angry fists in their faces, and the sheer weight of darkness that hangs over the land, believers here are ridiculed as fools in a lost cause. This uneven struggle reminds me of the lines of an old epic:

> Whither depart the souls of the brave
> that die in the battle,
> Die in the lost, lost fight,
> for the cause that perishes with them?"[4]

The difference for the brave souls here tonight is that Jesus is near, and his cause will never perish.

There was no electricity, just a few flickering lanterns, but that didn't lessen our joy. I thought of the words of Isaiah, "The people who walked in darkness have seen a great light" (9:2).

"The people who sat in darkness"

SOMEWHERE IN WESTERN INDIA

My last day with Aashish. We were up early, had prayer, and slipped out of town at first light to baptize five Christians. At least sixteen believers are ready for baptism, a serious step here in identifying with Christ. However, radical Hindus have imposed anticonversion laws in seven states, including this one; so to reduce visibility, believers are baptized in smaller groups in different places over the course of several weeks. Yesterday Aashish and two other pastors spent most of the afternoon scouting out a place for the baptism today, where we could avoid the police and their informants.

Believers are not told until the night before where to come for the baptism, because not only do the pastors risk interrogation, but a mob scene, too, if word gets out about where and when a baptism will take place. Swollen rivers in untried places add their own risks, and there have been drownings; so here a pastor sometimes needs to double as a lifeguard.

We all converged by jeep or motorbike to the appointed place, only to discover we weren't the first ones there. Villagers and water buffalo were taking their morning baths, and girls were scrubbing laundry along the riverbank. We quietly went further up the river and found another place. My brother Ramesh read Scripture, and Aashish baptized the believers in this remote river. Along the embankment we sang, "I have decided to follow Jesus, no turning back, no turning back."[5] Here that song means something!

After the baptisms, we went on to the meeting place for worship. The Christians here have sought for twelve years to acquire property for a church building and have been opposed at every turn. They have been harassed, beaten, and cheated, but they've continued to meet. The believers stood this morning to give thanks to the living God, who delivered them from their sins and the fear of dead idols. They lifted their voices (and every instrument they could find) in great praise. There was a harmonium, silver rattles called *gugra*, finger cymbals, tambourines, and my favorite, the *dholak*, a long drum played on both ends. Those without instruments used their hands, for no one wanted to be left out of this kingdom choir!

Perhaps because they have so few treasures, the one treasure— that Christ died for their sins and their lives are now forever bound up in his life—is all the more prized. My brothers and sisters are despised and rejected by those who call them Untouchables, yet they are loved and embraced by Jesus.

Afterward we took the Lord's Supper together. Aashish tore chapati into pieces, and we remembered the One torn for us. As the cup was poured into our hands, we remembered how Jesus was wounded for us, the marks in his hands the assurance that we are forever received, forever loved. And so this morning we shared in his sufferings and the fellowship of the cross—and together we echoed a distant song, a glimpse of things to come, as we sang "Alleluia! to the Lamb that was slain."

LAHORE, PAKISTAN

The *azan* blaring from several mosques like surround sound was my wake-up call just after five this morning. As the day went on, there would be many more reminders of Islam's sway here—sorrowful, black-and-blue ones.

All day long I sat with two Pakistani human rights lawyers, Joseph and Aneeqa, and Michele from Washington, DC, who serves on Capitol Hill as an advocate for persecuted Christians. For nine hours, in a little upstairs office off a narrow dusty alley in Lahore, Christians who were courageous enough—and able-bodied enough—came to tell their stories. We heard stories of robbery, rape, and murder at the hands of Muslims. We saw their scars and shared their tears.

About eight o'clock this evening Joseph drove us over to Lahore General Hospital to visit Pastor Indriaz, who was severely beaten by several Muslims in his village near Manawala yesterday. We walked through a dark courtyard, careful not to stumble over the people spending the night there. Families of patients huddled together in the shadows, sometimes spotted only by the clink of cooking pots or the orange glow of a cigarette.

In the hospital ward, forty men were housed with Pastor Indriaz. Cats darted in and out of the room, and flies lingered over the blood-spattered floor. The left side of the young pastor's head was smashed in. The beating severed his ear and left him blind in one eye. Because of convulsions, his wrists were awkwardly tied with cords, leaving him in a position of twisted agony. His wife, Shinaz, sat next to him, holding their three-month-old boy, Saman. She stared blankly at her husband with indescribable sadness in her eyes, as the baby nuzzled her and cried softly.

Joseph and Aneeqa confronted the doctors. It seems clear that the doctors had hoped Indriaz would be dead by now, and they are uncomfortable with the attention his case is now getting. Before I left, Indriaz began to stir and fixed his one eye on me. Who can describe the sorrow in that eye—or the anger I feel tonight?

SANGLA HILL, PUNJAB PROVINCE, PAKISTAN

Dust and ash stir in front of the charred face of a church firebombed last Saturday—its doors and windows now black, gaping wounds. We have spent the day here, walking among the burned churches and homes of Christians, and talking with the victims—and there are many. This past Saturday morning a Muslim mob of two thousand to three thousand, urged on by their imams, attacked Christians in their homes and firebombed five of their churches, their school, and even many of their homes. Hundreds of Christians, knowing a storm was about to break upon them, had fled the night before into the cane fields and the countryside. It was a night of shivering terror. Those left in Sangla Hill were caught up in a whirlwind of demon rage.

One courageous Christian named Zulfiqar brought families into his home and little courtyard. Believers huddled together, while Zulfiqar stood at his gate with a shotgun and a Kalashnikov. They all made it through that day safely, armed with prayer and cold steel. This tall, quiet hero doubtless saved lives and spared many girls from being raped. We met with some of the young girls who went through that night and day of burning and looting, their wide eyes still filled with fear and tears. We tried to comfort them as best we could. Before we left, Joseph prayed in Urdu and committed them to the Father's keeping, concluding with the Lord's Prayer. "Deliver us from evil" never meant as much as it did tonight.

Today I held men in my arms who sobbed uncontrollably from anguish and the bruises left by their police torturers. The Masih brothers told their story, while sitting in their smashed and looted home. This is a poor family, and what little they had is now destroyed or stolen, including a daughter's dowry. Their name is Masih, a common Christian surname in Pakistan. In the 1920s, when families were required to take a last name, many Christians took Masih, "a follower of Christ, the Masih—the Messiah." And so, it seems, their name makes them marked men.

Before leaving the city, we went to the police station. About thirty armed policemen gathered around us, while Joseph and I had a straight talk with the newly appointed police chief. I reminded him that hundreds of people were relying on his leadership to protect them and that the world was watching what he and his men would do. Of course, these are the same policemen who stood by and watched the riot—and the same ones who tortured the Masih brothers.

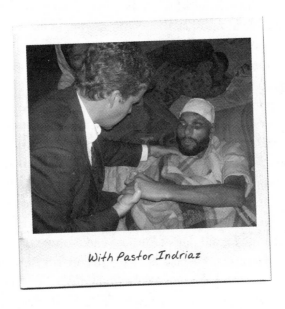

With Pastor Indriaz

A full moon rises over the cane fields around Sangla Hill, and in the twilight a minaret looks like a stake driven through the heart of this city. Three hundred Christian families live here, and not one of them feels safe tonight. My mind is swirling with all I've seen today—charred crosses, churches and homes gutted by fire, the cries of children, and the pleas of their parents for someone to protect them. The only comfort any of us have found today has been from the Scripture. Standing outside the charred remains of the Salvation Army Church, a believer named Gulzar came up to me to talk. His broken English was mended by a winning smile and joyful countenance. Gulzar told me that two promises helped him face the fear—and then he began to quote from John 14: "Let not your hearts be troubled. . . . In my Father's house are many rooms. If it were not so, would I have told you that I go to prepare a place for you? And if I go and prepare a place for you, I will come again and will take you to myself, that where I am you may be also" (14:1–3). And then my dear brother lifted my spirits and gave meaning to all I have witnessed today. "Be faithful unto death," Gulzar said, quoting our Lord, "and I will give you the crown of life" (Rev. 2:10).

LAHORE, PAKISTAN

This evening we returned to the hospital to check on Pastor Indriaz. Incredibly, the hospital had released him, saying he was in "satisfactory condition." We found him lying on some blankets on a concrete walkway outside the ward, with his discharge papers and a bottle of vitamins. His family was with him, but they didn't know what to do. It looks like Indriaz has lost the use of his right arm, his blind eye now white, and his ear badly stitched together. Most people would not treat a dog the way they have treated this man. While we talked to his mom, Indriaz looked up and began to sob. I held his hand, and Michele wiped his tears. Aneeqa explained to him that we were going to transfer him to a private medical facility for care. We will not leave him here to die.

LAHORE, PAKISTAN

In the shadow of a mosque, I gathered with Christians in the heart of Lahore. There were two thousand believers inside—and four thousand sandals outside! A string of deacons with metal detectors were positioned at the entrances, as a first line of defense against grenade bombings. I am now seated on the floor of a great room, the men on one side and the women on the other. It is a sea of joyful faces, accented with bright chadors on the women's side. Their songs of praise and songs of the Lamb drown out the drone of the Muslim call to prayer from the nearby mosque. Even in this dark land, God has his witnesses, and this morning they are singing.

They are lambs among wolves, but gathered together in this fold, in the presence of their Great Shepherd, there is comfort, and there is strength.

In this season of journeys and of sorrows, in places where only a little footing has been gained for the gospel after great sacrifice, when blood and tears and fear mark the passage, the Scriptures give me strength, where Paul said: "Do not lose heart. . . . We have this treasure in jars of clay, to show that the surpassing power belongs to God and not to us. We are afflicted in every way, but not crushed; perplexed, but not driven to despair; persecuted, but not forsaken. . . . As grace extends to more and more people it may increase thanksgiving, to the glory of God. So we do not lose heart" (2 Cor. 4:1, 7–9, 15–16).

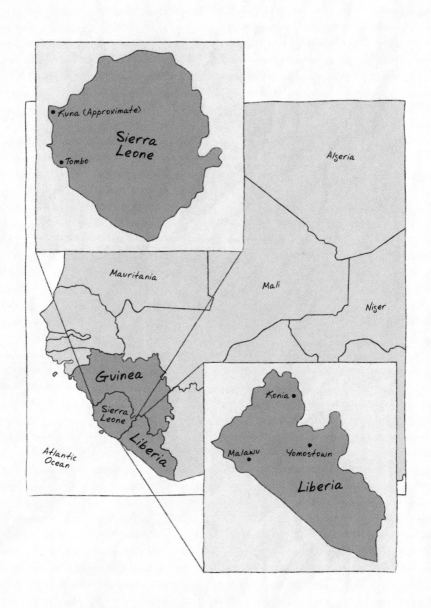

6
AMAZING GRACE

Liberia, Sierra Leone, and Guinea

Laundry girl, Liberia

The world is very different from the one in which William Carey, Adoniram Judson, and Hudson Taylor lived. They, along with other missionary trailblazers, inspired their generation to answer the Great Call. In the nineteenth and twentieth centuries, missionary ranks were filled mostly by those from the English-speaking world: British, American, and Canadian. As they crossed continents and cultures with the gospel, though, things changed. People of every nation, tongue, and tribe were saved through faith in Christ. Churches sprang up, and Christians in many lands began sharing the gospel with their own people.

At the same time, over the past century political boundaries have grown dramatically as global forces cracked the old world to pieces, creating a new Babel of nations. There were just over fifty independent countries at the beginning of the twentieth century—today there are nearly two hundred. As the number of countries has grown, so, too, have the political barriers to Western missionaries. Yet, not surprisingly, the gospel continues to advance because Christ is building his church, as he said he would! Tremendous growth in churches has taken place in parts of Latin America, Africa, and Asia—and is taking place largely through effective, indigenous evangelism.

I saw this firsthand in Liberia and Sierra Leone. Remarkable Christians in both those countries are leading, serving, discipling, and multiplying themselves in the lives of others. All this in countries wounded by war, steeped in demon worship and Islam, and divided a hundred ways—a patchwork of people groups barely stitched together by bad roads and worse governments.

Long before these countries' boundaries were drawn, this stretch of West Africa was simply called "Guinea" by Europeans. It was a center of trafficking in gold, ivory, and humans. Ironically, before Liberia and Sierra Leone became countries to resettle freed African slaves, this region had been a major source and transit point for the slave trade. John Newton was here. That was before John Newton, the godless, slave-ship captain, became John Newton, the pastor and hymn writer. Intervening grace made him a new man, as if he had been born a second time!

This amazing grace that John Newton wrote about in his day has been found by many here in West Africa in our day. The gospel is crossing borders and crushing barriers and giving sight to those who once were blind. In this corner of Christ's kingdom, a dress rehearsal is already underway for the day when the ransomed from every nation, tongue, and tribe will see their King, the King with scars on his hands. And they will sing—we will sing—for joy and wonder at the reach of such grace!

KONIA, NORTHERN LIBERIA

Left Monrovia early this morning. The Liberian capital is a sprawling, battered, crowded, seaside city. Monrovia and, in theory, all of Liberia was founded by Americans as a place to resettle freed African slaves; so the freedmen came from America and created a country much like the only one they had ever known. Liberia has a constitution that begins with "We the people" and a flag that looks like something Betsy Ross made. The African-American settlers, along with the missionaries that accompanied them, brought Christianity to Liberia. After 150 years, Monrovia has a church on practically every corner. But, as is often the case, comfort and corner lots stifled the further advance of the gospel. So the sixteen original tribes within the lines of Liberia remained mostly unreached, and Islam and demon worship held uncontested power over the millions of people who lived in the interior.

This gulf between Monrovia and the rest would have many other expressions as well, and by the 1990s, the divisions would be drawn in blood as Liberia sank into the chaos of fourteen years of civil war. When I hear accounts of the war, it seems that hell opened her mouth and demons took on flesh. During those years, the country was cursed with a succession of strongmen and their drug-laced armies of child soldiers, rapists, and murderers. One of them was the winsome "liberator" Charles Taylor, who ate the hearts of some of his choice victims after he came to power. This charismatic cannibal is now in prison at The Hague for crimes against humanity.[1]

The war left Liberia more of a crime scene than a battlefield. It was a war without rules, without winners, without purpose. The country's infrastructure was blown apart, and its conscience was stained with blood. So much suffering, so much atrocious killing, and yet the common killers who did those things have simply washed their hands, moved to the city, and taken up their business as usual. Some even traded their camos for a suit and a government office, as if nothing happened. So the silence of guilt and the silence of grief mingle in the streets—a kind of unspoken peace—over an unspeakable war.

Skittered along a red scrub-board of a road for eight hours today on the drive from Monrovia to the land of the Loma people in northern Liberia. As the crow flies, it isn't much more than a hundred miles. Unfortunately, I wasn't flying with the crows! Despite the road, I caught some sleep to add to the three hours I got last night. Dennis drove us today. My Liberian brother is a man in motion, combining joy with a tireless passion for the gospel. A pastor of pastors, a mentor of men, the Lord has used him to lead a church planting movement called Christian Revival Churches, which has grown from seven churches to sixty-two in three years—plus a couple dozen preaching points—a gospel vanguard of this frontline force.

Roland is here, too. He and Dennis make a great team. Dennis is the preacher. Roland is the well-driller—a combination of fire and water! Roland's life is itself a story of grace. He was fifty years old before he believed the gospel and received of the grace of God. Before that time, as he describes it, he had an empty hole in his life that he filled up with money and achievements. But no matter how many things he stuffed into that hole, it was always empty—until Christ filled his life! Now he's in West Africa drilling wells, bringing fresh water to people who before had only water contaminated with filth and disease. As wonderful as clean water is, it only gets better—because well-drilling has opened hearts to the gospel!

Before we reached Konia, Winston, one of Dennis's evangelists, stopped and got some snacks for us. A roadside hawker had little plastic bags filled with water and fresh, fat bamboo worms. Winston likes them raw and wriggling, so he was excited! But in deference to his less enthusiastic guests, he waited to fry and eat them when we got to Konia. They really aren't that bad, except for the head, which was kind of pokey—and which I spit out when no one was looking!

Besides introducing me to fried bamboo worms, Winston also

introduced me to a proper Liberian handshake. Handshakes here seem to have more moving parts than at home. First, each person grips the other's hand in the usual way. Then, in one fluid motion that follows, the hands shift to a soul shake position, then drawing back off each other's open hands, the shake finishes with a snap of the fingers. It's fun, and I'm already getting lots of practice—but I still need to work on the snap.

Konia is actually where Dennis grew up. God is using him mightily to reach his own people, the Loma, along with other tribes. To Dennis, Konia holds many emotions. His house was destroyed in the war, and, other than memories, the foundation is all that remains. Nearby is the place where his father was beheaded and his brother shot in the back by soldiers—hideous men who could laugh while they killed.

This evening Dennis and I walked around the village, which was busy with the basics: getting water, scrubbing off the dust of the day, making fire, and preparing rice, which is their "daily bread." The children helped, too, and seemed to know how to turn work into play as they threshed the swamp rice, stuffing it into sacks, and beating the daylights out of it with sticks. Palms and huts now seem silver as the moon rises above Konia. The shadows beneath are filled with the voices of a village getting ready for bed. Here waking and sleeping follow the sun; so I think I'll find a bed, too, before the sun turns up again.

KONIA, NORTHERN LIBERIA

Went out this morning around Konia village. At the edge of town is a thick stand of old trees. It's called "the Devil's Forest" because it is dedicated to the Devil. Most villages in this region practice demon worship and have these places. It's where men and boys go to learn the arts and sciences of Satan. It's where they are taught curses and offer sacrifices to demon spirits—it's a place of unspeakable darkness and evil. But when, by God's grace, demon worshippers become Christ followers, the darkness is swept away at light speed!

I met such a new man this morning. His name is Washington. He is a skilled carpenter who has a little shop along the main road of Konia. His "power tools" are hard hands and a sharp blade. Washington believed on the Lord and forsook the religion and company of demon worshippers. However, a committee of his old crowd came to beat and kidnap him, but he escaped their trap. When the plot was known, Pastor Dennis confronted the men and declared that if they struck Washington, they were lifting their hands against Washington's God. The message was clear: Don't mess with God! Conscious that they faced a greater One, they shrank back into their shadowy forest.

Washington spoke to me of the life and freedom he now has in Christ. He has learned to read his tribal dialect, so he was eager to read the Scripture to me in Loma. Knowing of the dark dungeon of his dark past, I asked Washington to read about light and deliverance. He read from John 9 of the man born blind who never saw light until Christ opened his eyes. The blind man's testimony to Jesus's power was as simple and clear as his sight, and Washington, too, can now say, "Though I was blind, now I see!"

Washington has helped build churches in village after village as the gospel has swept through Loma country. The gospel is setting people free, and in some of those towns, the high places, the Devil's forests, are coming down. There is even talk in Konia of cutting down the Devil's Forest. Perhaps one day the old trees that housed the demons will bend beneath Washington's blade and be fashioned into something beautiful.

Departed Konia late afternoon for Zagadeh, an unreached village up toward the border of Guinea. Winston led the way on his motorbike loaded down with his usual compact cargo: a projector, a screen, and even a small generator to power the showing of the JESUS film. The narrow road snaked through ragged, slash-and-burn fields into an old cocoa forest, darkened by the descending night. For the villagers, the day was drawing down and men with machetes were returning from the fields; but for us, our work was just beginning. Winston quickly assembled volunteers to help with the setup, mostly villagers who were curious and eager to help.

Winston chose the place for the showing—a perfect location on a hillside between the mosque and the Devil's Forest of Zagadeh. They hacked holes in the hard clay and planted the poles and hoisted the screen, like raising the flag on Iwo Jima. The battle lines were drawn. Dennis, Winston, and the evangelists gathered in a circle and prayed. They prayed forcefully like they were in a fight— which they were, for showing the JESUS film, the Gospel of Luke in living color, was a direct assault on hell's gate here. Hundreds gathered around the two-sided screen to see and hear the Gospel of Luke told in their tongue. At one point people in the crowd turned to one another and said, "Jesus is speaking Loma!"

At the crucifixion scene, Winston paused the film, and Dennis preached. Then the film continued, and the gospel story unfolded from the cross to the empty tomb. Afterward, Pastor Dennis invited people to receive the One who died for their sins, and the gates of hell did give way! About two hundred responded to the invitation, and the different evangelists that came for this evening's outreach gathered the people in groups and further explained the gospel to them. I thought of the words of Isaiah: "a nation that did not know you shall run to you" (Isa. 55:5).

Some of the evangelists stayed in Zagadeh overnight for more follow-up in the morning, and we returned to Konia late, with laughter and light hearts.

MALAWU, LIBERIA

We were up early. The sun, like me, was not awake as we walked over to church in Konia for the daily 5:30 prayer meeting. Dennis struck a makeshift church bell (an empty propane tank), calling Christians to rise and pray. In the distance, I saw a dot of light bouncing in the darkness and a woman's voice, clear and strong singing, "Good morning, Jesus. Good morning, Lord." About twenty Christians gathered this morning at the Konia church, and the meeting began with praise to God who made the day. "This is the day that the LORD has made" (Ps.118:24). Well, he had not quite made it yet, but we were all anticipating it.

Afterward, went on toward the Guinea border to two new gospel plants at Borkeza and Kpassagezia. Roland needed to scout out places for well-drilling, and Dennis wanted to see the progress of the church buildings. It was beautiful to see a bamboo cross raised over a village for the first time. Dennis learned his church planting methods from the book of Acts. They pray, fast, and then send evangelists in by twos to tell the good news. Dennis said they target the toughest villages, the strongest strongholds of Satan, and there they pursue the most obstinate among the village leaders—men who give new meaning to the phrase "chief of sinners." When these men fall down before the cross, it opens a floodgate. Within six months or so, a church typically moves through three "building phases." They first meet under a tree. Then they build a bamboo hut with simple pole benches—and then they pack it out. The one in Borkeza had over seventy-five people this past Sunday. The roofs of these bamboo churches are made from banana leaves skillfully stitched together. Such shingles last for only about a year, but the people have moved on to the next stage long before then—a more permanent meeting place. Dennis always encourages the believers not to wait around for any help from the outside but to begin to make and collect the thousands of bricks it will take for their permanent building. Here bricks are made with mud with rice straw as a binder and then baked in the sun. Dennis told me that mud bricks are cheaper and cooler than cinder blocks—and they have the added advantage of stopping bullets better. This is no small consideration in this place.

So new believers put their backs into the work from the beginning. But also from the beginning, they look beyond their village to the next village—even to the next country. Kpassagezia is the end of the line in Liberia, but beyond it is the border of Guinea. People from Guinea already come by bush path to Kpassagezia. They have heard and received the gospel, but they need their own church—and all of Guinea needs to be reached. A road is being cut out of the jungle from Kpassagezia to the border two miles away, opening the way for trade and truth.

Children in Kpassagezia, as in every African village, are everywhere, and they greeted us enthusiastically. These children are too poor and live too far out to go to school, so we took a walk together down the new road. I wish I could have walked with them all the way to Guinea, for beyond that border is another border—that of the old Mali kingdom and Timbuktu, from which Islam was first thrust into these parts long ago. In those unreached lands, there are more foundations to be laid, more lives to be changed, and more bamboo crosses to be raised.

Drove on to Zorzor, where we stripped our truck and packs down to essentials and then took the rough road into the bush. When the road ended, we left the vehicle for the long hike up the mountain of Malawu. As we walked along, the path took us over log footbridges, rivulets of army ants, and towering Entlike trees.

The story of Malawu is almost unbelievable. Malawu was the "Mecca" of spirit worship in all of Liberia. This mountaintop town was founded by a witch long ago, and such demon powers dwelled here that even presidents of Liberia would come here to seek special powers and curses against their enemies. Animal—and even human—sacrifices were offered here. If there was ever a gate to hell, Malawu was that gate. It was literally considered sacred ground, and so in the debauched worship of the Devil, shoes had to be removed and women had to remove their blouses before entering the gates to the town. It was a place of unspeakable evil and violent darkness.

But about two years ago, a man from Malawu came down from this mountain, heard the gospel, and believed on Jesus. He and Dennis and the evangelists began to pray. What followed was nearly a year of praying and fasting in preparation for the gospel assault on Malawu. Many tried to discourage them. Some of Dennis's friends begged him not to go, saying he was going into a death trap. But Dennis fixed his heart on the Lord and not his fears, and just over a year ago they came up the mountain in faith. What they found was amazing! They were received by the elders who heard their witness for Christ and declared to them, "Our hearts and hands are open to you—even if you want to build a church here!" When the village people heard that, they were so happy they began to dance with joy that they could have a place to worship the true God. They circled the hilltop with joyful dancing and singing. I had heard about this "Malawu Miracle" from Dennis, but I still was not prepared for what I saw when I reached the summit: there before me was the cross! The church building now stands on ground once dedicated to Satan.

A Christian lady named Kulbah was the first to greet us. The marks of her transformed life could be seen on her beautiful countenance, by her beautiful dress, and by shoes on her feet! Now she is a free woman walking over the ground that Satan long ago usurped but which has now been reclaimed for Christ. These people were never meant to worship demons, were never meant for prison—they were made in God's image and Christ has rescued and redeemed them. In just over a year, the high altar where animal and human sacrifices were made has been overturned, and half the village has turned from darkness to light—and the light shines in their faces, for they are now sons and daughters of the King!

Roland just loaned me his satellite phone to call home. Standing under the night sky, it was good to talk to Debbie and to hear her voice again. Looking up into a magnificent canopy of stars, I said to her, "I see Orion." She replied, "You see a lion?!" And then the signal went dead. I couldn't leave it there, with everything the imagination could add to that. So I climbed on a tree for a better signal and called back to assure her the biggest animal I've seen thus far was a goat! So this day ends as it began, beneath the stars.

YOMOSTOWN, LIBERIA

The days here are passing—a succession of bush trails and gospel breakthroughs. It reminds me of Hudson Taylor's motto, "Always advancing."[2] The gospel *is* advancing on all fronts! I saw it vividly in Malawu and in all the days since.

Before we left Malawu, the village women brought us coffee—it was strong and black and perfect for shaking off the short night. Dennis and I had a good time talking over our morning coffee. He's like a long-lost brother, and the Lord has knit our hearts together during these days. I would have liked to have stayed longer, but the sun was burning off the mist that draped the Loma plains below us—and so we moved on to get a head start on the heat, since we had a two-hour hike back down to the jeep. Before parting ways at the foot of the mountain, we all joined in prayer, asking that Malawu would continue to be a "city set on a hill" so that gospel light would shine to all the surrounding villages greater than the darkness that once crept out of it.

Took a break in Zorzor. We repacked our gear and then took the long, dusty road to Jawajeh in the heart of Gola country in western Liberia. The Gola tribe is predominantly Muslim and was largely unreached until three years ago. That's when evangelists, nurses, and Roland's well-drillers joined forces to bring the good news to the Gola in Jawajeh. They held village medical clinics, dug wells, and brought the message of the gospel—and many believed! Now there are four churches and eight preaching points scattered among the Gola, with the number of Christians now nearly a thousand throughout the region.

One of the men who brought the gospel here is now the youth pastor at the church at Jawajeh. What can I say about Johnny? Johnny loves Jesus, Johnny loves kids, and Johnny has never walked. He was born a cripple, and his mother used to weep over him. In this society, his prospects were utterly hopeless—just a roadside beggar, just something to spit at. But Johnny had a friend who carried him on his back to church, and there Johnny received

Christ—and then everything changed in his young heart. He no longer looked at his useless legs as a curse but as a gift from God, for Johnny came to understand that the Father always blesses and never harms his children. It was tender to hear Johnny tell how before he got a wheelchair, he tried to ease his mother's pain and show her his love for God by washing the dishes, which he would collect as he dragged himself on the ground and then wash in a bucket. It was a beginning of a lifetime of serving others and Jesus with all his strength.

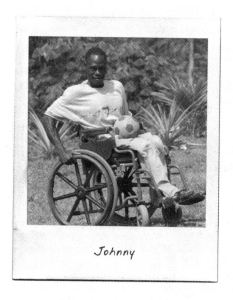

Johnny

Afterward, Johnny's oldest son pushed his dad in the wheelchair to the little hilltop near the church, and Johnny clanged the "church bell," an empty propane tank. As he gathered children to the church from all over town, I thought of the Lord's parable where the master said to his servant, "'Go out quickly to the streets and lanes of the city, and bring in the poor and crippled and blind and lame.' And the servant said, 'Sir, what you commanded has been done, and still there is room.' And the master said to the servant, 'Go out to the highways and hedges and compel people to come in, that my house may be filled'" (Luke 14:21–23).

From his wheelchair, Johnny can see so clear and far. He sees beyond his brokenness, beyond this broken world, to the One who was broken for him and who will someday give Johnny legs to run to him. I believe Johnny will be a sprinter in that day. In the new heaven and the new earth, the new Johnny will run rings around Saturn!

One of the keys to the breakthrough to the Gola people, as well as other West African tribes, has been providing clean drinking water, which opens up wider doors for witness. God raised up Roland for this purpose. He and his Liberian team have drilled hundreds of wells in the past five years. Each well serves about four hundred people in a village; so the number of people who have been given fresh water is staggering—tens of thousands.

Went out with him to drill yet another well in this dry and thirsty land. It was so dry and sandy that one of the drilling trucks got bogged down. Nevertheless, after a bit of push and pull, we made it through and set up the drill. Roland was in his element—organizing his team, patching, improvising, and pulling through. He was always in the thick of the action, his servant's hands covered with sweat, dirt, and diesel. The people of the village helped where they could by digging the pits and lining them with clay slurry, which held the water needed for drilling. They even provided coconuts to refresh us.

We sank the drill, and after only four hours, we found water—at just forty feet! It gushed out! It was cool and sweet. Empty buckets suddenly appeared from all directions. Roland filled them, and then turned the hose on the children who had never played in water before. There was so much splashing and laughing, and so many brimming buckets, at a place that was just another stretch of dust a few hours earlier. The water was down there all along—someone just had to make a way to get to it. The same is true of unreached people. Roland, teaming up with Liberian Christians, is bringing the Water of Life to village after village, for he knows from the woman of Samaria that wells are good places for thirsty sinners to meet Jesus.

"*Empty buckets suddenly appeared.*"

Today is the Lord's Day, and it caps a week of following the gospel trails of Africans reaching Africans. I've seen firsthand that one of the hardest parts of reaching unreached people is simply getting to them. It seems obvious, but the biggest reason people remain unreached is because no one has reached them, no one has gone deep into the jungle to find them and tell them about Jesus. The roads to reach them are rough and sometimes risky, and the bridges are riskier. Often we have gotten out of the truck, crossed a stream on foot, and then prayed as Dennis threaded his way over a shaky bridge. And so, we have our own version of the old song "Bridge over Troubled Water"—it's called "troubled bridge over water"!

Traveled over such bridges and roads today with Dennis and his wife Vania and some Christians from Jawajeh. We traveled to worship with a brand-new band of believers meeting in a little mud-and-stick church building in the Gola village of Yomostown. Out here in the bush, there is an 80 percent illiteracy rate, so the pastors emphasize systematic Bible-story teaching—working through the Scripture chronologically—along with an open exchange of questions to deepen the people's understanding of the unfolding story from creation to Christ. Their songs joyfully reflect these great Bible stories—like Miriam and her companions' songs did after crossing the Red Sea, when the people danced and sang and took up tambourines. Only here among the Gola, worshippers take up a gourd rattle called a *sassa*. One of the women played this rattle, and the only other instruments were our hands and feet. We stirred up quite a bit of dust! My favorite song was called "The Horn of Jericho." In Gola they sang of how the Lord brought the walls of Jericho down. It was fun to mime the horn and remember such a victory! And though we are from such different worlds, beneath the cross we're one by the grace of God.

As I sit at this distant outpost of Christ's kingdom, I recall Jesus's words: "I am the good shepherd. . . . I lay down my life for the sheep. And I have other sheep that are not of this fold. I must bring them also, and they will listen to my voice. So there will be one flock, one shepherd" (John 10:14–16).

KUNA, SIERRA LEONE

Set out for the Sierra Leone border at first light. Dennis greeted the morning with song, which cheered us over another rough road. Sierra Leone has the worst poverty, worst infant mortality rates, worst corruption—and worst roads. The roads are of unrelenting badness. Took one such road out to the village of Kru. Dennis is a good jungle driver. If he weren't, I'd still be there. Went on until the road ended—and then walked on. After a short time, the land turned to sand. I passed women with baskets of dried fish. Somehow, though, I wasn't prepared for what came next: the huddle of huts we were walking through suddenly parted and the ocean spread before us—the ends of the earth was also the end of the earth! The white edge of the ocean swept the shore, where dugouts and fishnets were scattered along the edge of the surf. Since wood, sticks, and even mud are hard to come by in this land of sand, the Kru people are masters of necessity, building their houses out of palm branches. The gospel was first brought here by a Liberian fisherman, and the Christians have recently built a church, also of palm branches. I guess every Sunday is Palm Sunday here. The believers were very kind to us. They prepared a meal of fish gravy over rice, along with succulent yellow oranges, which refreshed us for the long, long journey into the interior of Sierra Leone.

Our guide here in Sierra Leone is Pastor Alphonso. His help has been invaluable in getting us through this broken land. This is his broken world, so he knows how to put enough of the pieces together to get by—whether it's negotiating passage of a remote river or crossing countless checkpoints where some local entrepreneur makes a living by holding up vehicles. But Alphonso is also a man of gospel vision. He knows firsthand the radical rescue work that sets prisoners free and gives sight to blind men, because Jesus brought him out of the dark prison of Islam.

Alphonso is a Fula, from the proud tribe that brought Islam to West Africa many centuries ago. He was a zealous Muslim who gave the first call to prayer of the day from the mosque. One day he was told there was a man preaching Christ in his town. He found him and struck and cursed him. The Christian responded with kindness and tears and said to Alphonso, "I will pray that your eyes will be opened." Alphonso said, "What? Do you think I am blind?" and walked away. That night, before Alphonso was to get up and give the call to prayer, he was awakened by a voice, the words of Scripture, the words of Christ: "Come unto me, come unto me, come unto me." Alphonso called out in the dark, "Who is there?" He lit a candle to see, but no one was there. Suddenly he was struck with great fear, and he remembered the words of the young man, "I will pray that your eyes will be opened." Knowing where there was a church, he went to it, and there the pastor led him to Christ.

Alphonso became bold in declaring his faith to his family, and as a result was utterly rejected by them. His aunt even tried to kill him by poisoning him. Though the poison was powerful, the Lord spared his life, to the amazement and disgust of his family.

Later the Lord brought a wonderful lady into his life named Nana, who also came to Christ out of Islam. Together they have spearheaded a rapidly reproducing church-planting movement reaching deep into Sierra Leone, even as far as the border with Guinea. In the past few days, I've seen new churches that have sprung up among fishermen, farmers, and soldiers. As in Liberia, the gospel is penetrating Islam's territory here in Sierra Leone—the cross over the crescent! But it's not without violent opposition. One church building I saw in Samu was recently destroyed by a mob, stirred up by a village elder when his own son became a Christian. Such attacks are just part of the price, and Christians here don't seem too worried about fighting over buildings. They know better than most that bricks are just so much mud. The gospel advance would be slowed down—even stalled—if they concerned themselves too much with buildings.

Despite the opposition, the testimony of believers is gaining ground, shaking hell's gates here. In this part of West Africa, Islam and spirit worship are often inextricably linked, and so the people also sacrifice animals and worship demons, some of which they believe reside inside sacred trees. Near the town on the banks of the Kolenté River was a huge cottonwood tree that was twice as large and tall as the others. It was a place of sacrifice and worship, and the townspeople feared the evil spirits that resided in the tree. When Alphonso and some of the other evangelists came into the town a couple of years ago, the people began complaining that the tree was losing its power. By the time Roland and his well-drillers came, there was an uproar when it was determined that because of the presence of the Christians, the spirits had left the tree. Then a couple of months ago, a big wind blew in one night and took the tree down! Though there were many trees along that river delta, this was the only one that fell. Today the townspeople are cutting

175

it up and using it for firewood! "Who is like you, O LORD, among the gods? Who is like you, majestic in holiness, awesome in glorious deeds, doing wonders?" (Ex. 15:11).

I'm in Kuna, near the border with Guinea. Some Guineans have crossed the border here for trade and have heard the good news, proving once again that the gospel is not bound by lines on a map. Still, though, Alphonso wants to see churches established in Guinea, starting with the town of Pamlap. Alphonso has made contact with the chief there, who will meet us at the border. Alphonso went to that town a few months ago but was told to get out. Today we try again.

The gospel without borders! We had no visas for Guinea, no permission to cross the border; but when the chief, whose name is Mohammed Lamin-Sesay, arrived, he took personal responsibility for us and directed the guards to let us pass. So Mohammed on a motorcycle led us into this new country!

Mohammed on a motorcycle

Pamlap is a dusty, dreary place, brightened by people wearing colorful silk and brilliant patterns of African *kente* cloth. Mohammed led us into the heart of the town. Soon an impromptu council of elders was assembled, including the imam from the nearby mosque. Formalities and gifts of peace were exchanged. Alphonso declared the chief to be a man of peace, and the chief reminded the elders that Alphonso had once lived in this city when he was a boy. So they welcomed him as a "son of the soil." Yet Alphonso went on to explain that though he was a son of the soil, he was also now a Christian and wanted to start a church there. Discussions went back and forth in a marvelous mosaic of languages (Fulani, Susu, French, and English). Nana, recalling a language she hadn't spoken in years—Susu—was a vital link in carrying on and connecting the discussions.

It was a jaw-dropping moment when the old Muslim elders agreed that a church could be built in their town, and one added, "We are ready for you to wake us up!" Another leader said afterward, "Guinea is ready for the gospel!"

We returned to the border before nightfall with great joy that the same God who opened the Red Sea for Moses and opened prison gates for Peter and Paul, opened a way for us, too!

TOMBO, SIERRA LEONE

Our last day. Set out for Plaintain Island, twenty miles out in the Atlantic. Plaintain Island was a major transit point in the slave trade, the last bit of Africa that uncounted thousands of Africans would ever see before being crammed into the holds of ships for the passage to the Americas. The island is also a big part of the John Newton story. It was there he was made a slave of slaves. Later, after "many dangers, toils, and snares," he returned to Plaintain Island, where he in soul agony crept to a remote shore of the island to pray for saving mercy. By grace, he was never the same. And so Roland and I wanted to explore Plaintain Island. Alphonso and Nana wanted to see it as well because the people there speak Temne, the language of Nana's people. They hope to see a church there someday.

Tombo, Sierra Leone

Through a friend of a friend, an officer gave permission that a crew of the Sierra Leone Navy would take us to the island in a patrol boat. I'll have to say that my idea of a navy patrol boat was quite different than the little twenty-foot skiff we boarded. We knew we were in trouble when we were only two miles out, the engine was sputtering, and we began to take on water. Overloaded with fuel and passengers, we were only making ten knots. There was some question about whether we should keep going, but the skipper reassured us that we would make it, and I sided with him to press on. By the time we were three miles out, things went from bad to worse, and Roland wisely overruled and insisted that we go back. We continued to take on water from the stern and from a crack that now appeared in the hull. Hampered by a headwind, we put in at the nearest shore at Tombo, with little time to spare.

There on the shore were hundreds of people waiting to crowd onto other boats bound for the island. Four months ago, one of these boats went down here in these perilous waters. Over two hundred perished, including seventy schoolchildren. Most of the victims were never retrieved. They were just gone—lost and lost.

The captain, it is reported, had given the passengers assurance that all was well, even though the sea was frightening and he was drunk. Then the storm struck with full force. I can only imagine the cries and terror—and then the awful silence. The force of their silence breaks my heart. We had a near miss today over that watery grave. I know I am safe in Christ. I know the only danger I faced today was drowning. But standing on the shore with the waiting crowd, I was overcome with the sudden uncertainty of all we see—on this side of the thin line of life. As I mingled with the others, the sun felt good, and the hour was a gift.

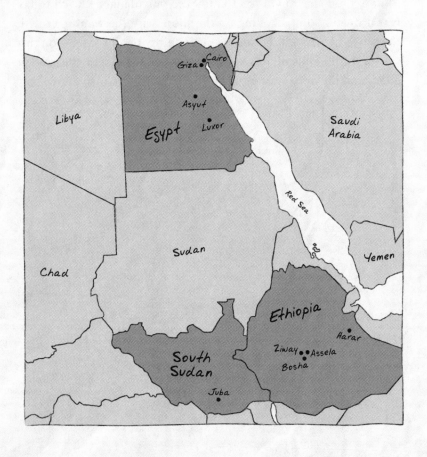

7
PRISON BREAK

The Horn of Africa and Egypt

An Oromo shepherdess,
Great Rift Valley, Ethiopia

Islam is a prison. The call to prayer, which blares five times a day from minarets that are ominously reminiscent of guard towers, is like roll call in a gulag. But that is the view from the outside. Inside, it is such a big prison, that many of its people live and die in the shadows, unaware of the walls. A few, though, see light beyond the bars, and they dare to test their chains and reach out. For those Muslims, there are laws to keep them inside—laws that promise death to those who "change" their religion.

In Egypt and parts of the Horn of Africa, laws and society are violently opposed to conversion to Christianity. Believers may face beatings, torture, prison—and that's just what the government does; family members may go straight for the kill. By contrast, conversion to Islam is very, very easy. One simply has to repeat the *shahada* or "testimony." It's just eight simple words in Arabic: "*La ilaha illa Allah, wa-Muhammad rasul Allah.*" ("There is no god but Allah, and Mohammed is his prophet.") Then instantly you have jumped to "the other side" with all the privileges of membership—with one great exception; you can't go back, unless you want to die. Remember, you are in the prison now.

During my time in Ethiopia, Sudan, and Egypt I met men and women who by the grace of God have escaped the prison house of Islam, but it has cost them dearly. One young mother in Cairo, who had a two-year-old daughter and a five-month-old son, went to jail for nearly a year simply because she became a Christian. In other areas of Egypt and the Horn, Christians have been massacred by Islamic terror groups—run down in the streets and shot like animals.

However, the word of the Lord to Moses is still true today across these lands: "I have surely seen the affliction of my people which are in Egypt, and have heard their cry by reason of their taskmasters. I know their sufferings" (Ex. 3:7). Christ has set his saving, sympathetic love on his people and on those still in prison. The gospel is powerful in breaking the bars, and men and women by the thousands are now stumbling out into the light.

HARAR, ETHIOPIA

Flew out yesterday from the Ethiopian capital of Addis Ababa to Harar. Tonight the *azan* falls with the shadows over the old walls of Harar. The chatter in the street is of a day gone by. I've found a place here for the night—a little whitewashed guesthouse that, except for electricity, has hardly changed in five centuries. A pomegranate tree graces the courtyard and offers a place of refuge and writing.

Set out this morning to explore this thousand-year-old caravan town. The streets are narrow, winding with cobbled stones polished by centuries of sandal-wear. Found the palace of the old king Haile Selassie. After he was murdered by the Communists in the 1970s, his houses were looted and occupied, but now this one is being restored as a museum. I coaxed the caretaker to let me go up to the king's balcony for a better view of the city. Minarets mark the landscape, a reminder of Islam's long-held claims here. In fact, Harar is considered the fourth holiest city of Islam—after Mecca, Medina, and Jerusalem. Being on the route of caravans and armies from the mouth of the Red Sea, Harar was, for Mohammed's followers, the gateway into the Horn of Africa.

Afterward, walked to the market. Along the way, passed the butcher's shop, where fresh camel hung on hooks and sharp knives were making short work of it. Here camels are as common as cows. Brown Harari eagles wheeled above, hoping for a bite of humpback. One of the butchers tossed up a scrap or two, creating quite an air show.

At the old city gate, crowds converged on a melee of markets. It was a wonderful assault on the senses. The spice market was in such close quarters that it was like climbing through a spice rack stuffed with sacks of mint, pepper, ginger, and brilliant white salt crystals dug out of the Danakil Depression, the hottest point in Africa just north of here. Nearby, the vegetable market was aswirl with Arabs and Abyssinians and with strange tongues and brilliant colors. The women's *shashs* (headcoverings) were not just blue, yellow, and red but were the richness of a painter's palette—azure, gold, and vermilion, all splashed against the canvas of mounds of melons, potatoes, onions, and okra.

Allan is with me here—a friend and brother who is passionate about the gospel and its advance in Ethiopia. This afternoon we met with several of the men he has been training: Meko, Fikra, and Thomas. These are humble men with the strength to do hard things—like walking into Muslim villages near Somalia and proclaiming Christ. These are areas where *al-Shabab*, Somalia's version of al-Qaeda, has infiltrated. *Al-Shabab's* signature brand of Islam includes kidnapping, piracy, and cutthroat devotion to Allah. And so, when these evangelists go into such lawless regions armed with the JESUS film and a backpack projector, it's like an act of war. They have risked death many times for Christ's sake.

I was quietly rebuked by how seriously they take God's Word in a life-and-death kind of way. Recently, hounded, hungry, and alone, Thomas nearly turned back. But he read Paul's letter to Timothy: "Endure suffering, do the work of an evangelist, fulfill your ministry" (2 Tim. 4:5). And so, Thomas again shouldered his cross and quickened his pace because he didn't want to be like Jonah: though he had "kingdom feet" (since he did finally go to Ninevah), he didn't have a "kingdom heart"—one that loved mercy and grace for his enemies. Thomas wanted to have kingdom feet *and* a kingdom heart.

Before we parted, Allan prayed for these brothers. He took us to the foot of the cross, to the only place where the sacrifices that these men and their wives are making make any sense.

Meko invited us to his home afterward for some Ethiopian hospitality. His wife Aster honored us with an Ethiopian coffee ceremony, which is an elaborate presentation that includes popcorn and burning sweet incense called *ogardin*. The heart of the ceremony, though, is the coffee—roasting the beans over charcoal, crushing them, and brewing them in a clay pot.

Ethiopia claims the honor as the birthplace of coffee—the word itself is derived from the Ethiopian region of Kaffa. Here, place names like Harar, Yirgacheffe, and Sidamo are, to the connoisseurs of caffeine worldwide, labels for fine brew. Actually, Arabia also lays claim to being the cradle of coffee, but today, savoring Aster's fresh, smooth cup, I have no doubt as to who has first honors! Our fellowship in the gospel was sweet, and so was our time as we prayed and parted ways.

Harar has been a crash course in Ethiopian culture and a powerful introduction to the hard edge of gospel work among the Muslim tribes here. Before leaving Harar, though, I had to find the Hyena Man. The Hyena Man feeds wild hyenas that come outside the city walls at night. After asking around, I found the bizarre ritual. A young man named Abbas was feeding strips of goat meat off a stick to a pack of about twenty hyenas, and for a few coins I was able to join in the fun. It was amazing to be so close that I could feel their hot breath in my face. They are warglike with thick necks and sharp jaws, and we all had a good laugh when it was over.

ASELA, ETHIOPIA

Took a ten-hour drive from Harar to Asela as we made our descent into the Great Rift Valley, the grand gash that cuts through the heart of Ethiopia. It was like flipping through an issue of *National Geographic,* with constantly changing terrain and vistas. The mountain air was aromatic with cedar and fragrant, mouth-watering eucalyptus trees. The hills were flowing with a brilliant yellow bloom called *meskel,* which is only out briefly this time of year. Good timing, for I wouldn't want to miss this!

As we continued our descent, though, the color drained out of the land as we reached the plains of Awash, which are wide, flat, and hot as a frying pan. Huge dust devils swirled across the barrenness. I saw a shepherd and his flock overtaken by a tornado of sand. Their cowering forms briefly silhouetted against the vortex before disappearing into it.

Our road then cut through the cratered remnants of old volcanoes that have left heaps of lava and deep pools and lakes. This land of fire and water draws a menagerie of birds and herds of camels, which fill their backpacks with water before setting out on their desert march.

Reached Asela in early evening, where my friend Michael ministers to orphans and broken people. Michael is a gracious brother, whose graciousness flows from grace. His life is a story of the gospel, of how Jesus can save the most unlikely sinners, and of how, because of such grace, they can, in turn, love the most unlikely.

Michael was born to a poor family in a poor village, but he got a chance to go to school, where he excelled. At seventeen, he was conscripted to fight in Ethiopia's war with Somalia. He quickly proved himself in combat and was then tapped to be a frontline commander in Ethiopia's brutal war with Eritrean separatists. Those were the years of Mengistu, a tyrant who overthrew the monarchy, murdered the king, and, backed by Soviet arms and MiGs, ruled Ethiopia with an iron fist.

Michael was a good Communist and a rising star in the regime. He was, in fact, part of a select group chosen to go to the Soviet Union to learn how to strengthen Communism's grip on the minds of the people. Ironically, the time in Moscow had the opposite effect, and he was disillusioned by the hollowness of it all. When Michael returned to Ethiopia, the country was descending into what became known as the Red Terror, when Mengistu, in the paranoia of power, purged every threat, real or imagined. Tens of thousands of Ethiopians, mostly young people, were murdered gangland style over a period of a year. Every morning Michael walked past fresh corpses, and his sense of justice was shattered. He joined a plot that was quietly taking shape to overthrow Mengistu. When the plot became known, most of the officers were executed. Michael escaped, and for three months he made his way across the forbidding terrain of southern Ethiopia, narrowly escaping death time and time again—death from Mengistu's men, death from lions, and death from hunger. Eventually he made it across the border to Kenya. And at the age of twenty-one, he found himself living on the streets of Nairobi—a homeless, nameless refugee.

After several months he met a pastor, who wasn't repulsed by his filthy condition. The pastor not only gave him a meal but the gospel, too—and Michael believed! Michael eventually found refuge in Canada and wasn't able to return to Ethiopia for years, until after Mengistu fell in 1991. When he was finally able to come back, he found that the Red Terror had left a million orphans. One evening as Michael was out walking, he heard a pleading voice, "Father, give me bread." It was a little orphan boy, perhaps five years old, one of the thousands living on the streets of Addis at the time. Somehow this particular child captured his heart. He gave him some money for food and asked him to come back in the morning.

That night Michael couldn't sleep. He lay in his bed and thought of that child sleeping on the street. Early in the morning he went out searching for the boy, but he couldn't find him. He searched the next day, too, but he never saw the boy again. I think the boy's voice still haunts him—and it changed his life and the lives of the hundreds of orphans Michael has rescued and raised over the past twenty years. Michael didn't set out to oversee the care, feeding, and education of hundreds of orphans. He simply answered the plea of a hungry, homeless child, and God opened his heart and his hands wider and wider.

ASELA, ETHIOPIA

Dusk is settling over Asela. It's the dissolution of the day and a good time to mix coffee with ink. This morning Michael took me to meet the AIDS orphans. Yerus and her little friend Lamrot met us at the gate. Yerus, which is short for "Jerusalem," came here when she was four. Michael found her at the hospital—an orphan with full-blown AIDS, waiting to die. She had lost her hair, and her head was covered with sores instead. Michael made a little *shash* for her and took her out shopping for clothes. Afterward he determined he had to help her. Because she was the first child with AIDS that he had ever taken into the orphanage, his heart was filled with fear and uncertainty. Still though, two things were certain: left alone, Yerus would soon die; and Michael had to do something.

So Jerusalem would be the beginning of taking care of AIDS orphans. Four years later, she has beautiful hair, which she had pulled back in a ponytail, and she has a strong faith and love for Jesus. There were seven other AIDS orphans at the orphanage when I visited. Michael said the children are the best therapy for each other—they take care of each other.

They all have their stories. Met Lamrot's brother, Nathaniel. When their mother died, Lamrot was one and her brother just four, but he took care of her until Michael learned of their plight and brought them here. Tamrat was found at the breast of his dead mother, who had died two days earlier. Tamrat's name means "miracle," but it seemed to me that there were eight miracles swirling around the yard—miracles of what gospel-driven love can do. Miracles like the little girl full of sores and left for dead now showing off her ponytail and winning my heart with her smile.

Many of these children have sponsors in the West to help fund their care and education. Michael doesn't refuse people who want to help a child, but he doesn't encourage it either. He said that sponsorships are a "good fund-raising strategy," but it's not sustainable. What Michael really wants is to turn the individual into a resource rather than just turning their need into a resource.

I got a glimpse of how he's doing that when we went from the homes to the shops. This place is called Christian Horizons—well named, for "horizon" speaks to me of vision and hope. Besides the various homes where the children and their caregivers live, there's a dairy farm, brick kiln, welding shop, and wood shop.

Visited the wood shop where men have been trained as furniture makers. Rough-hewn logs were being planed into boards—there is no question they use solid wood here! Several of the men are deaf. Michael says "disability" does not mean "inability." With training and a chance, these men are supporting themselves and the ministry here. But Michael is also pushing them to improve. Michael is a bit like me—he probably can't build a birdhouse, but he knows excellence; so he encourages the men along so that the creations of their hands reflect their Creator. These brothers of mine give testimony to the One who loved the deaf. On the wall of their shop they have written in Amharic the question that is without question: "Who is like our God?" It's a beautiful boast drawn from the Psalms, a passage whose truth these men know very well: "Who is like the LORD our God? . . . He raises the poor from the dust and lifts the needy from the ash heap" (Ps. 113:5, 7).

While the saws were blazing, just next door my friend Allan was rightly dividing the Word of truth. Christian Horizons is not only rescuing children but is also a force in strengthening the church in the radical rescue work of the gospel. Intensive Bible training was underway with men and women from all over the region—from elder statesmen like Pastor Ti-yay, who was tortured for his faith during the Communist era, to young men and women eager to learn and to share the Scriptures. Some of the pastors have said that in the past their only models for preaching were the "health and wealth" types they saw on television—an embarrassing American export. These same men are now getting a taste for simple, solid, biblical exposition, and they have publicly repented of how they handled God's Word before. What is so effective about the teaching that Allan is doing is that this learning is not for accumulation, but for multiplication. Allan is just the initiator of a movement—for this school has legs! These pastors and evangelists are in turn teaching other pastors and evangelists in ever widening circles of Ethiopians training Ethiopians in Word-centered preaching. I love to remember the Ethiopian in the book of Acts who searched the Scriptures; the Lord sent along Philip to show him Christ, whom he embraced in faith and joy. The Ethiopian eunuch surely brought the gospel back to this very land. Now in our time, God is raising up a new generation of Philips and of Ethiopians hungry to know and preach Jesus—to shake every corner of their nation with the gospel!

Before leaving Asela, I wanted to see Tariku. A few months back I heard about this eleven-year-old boy's remarkable rescue story. No one knows who his father or mother are. He just lived in the open like an animal—quite literally. The people in his town said he was smart, a survivor, because at night he slept with the wild dogs as protection from the hyenas. When Michael heard about the boy, he went out and found him. The sight and smell of a boy who had never bathed didn't turn him away—just the opposite. He took him in, loved him, clothed him, and named him. Today when I visited, Tariku was working on his first-grade math homework, and we chatted a bit to practice his English. Then he showed me his room where he bunks with two other orphan boys. Even now it makes me tear up to think about it. Tariku sat on his bed, the only bed he has ever known. Less than a year ago, he was sleeping on the ground with the dogs. It was precious and humbling to see such grace on display. Michael is Jesus's hands to these children, answering over and over a plea he heard long ago: "Father, give me bread."

Michael with Tariku

BOSHA, ETHIOPIA

Left Asela early for another descent into the Great Rift Valley. Before the road from Asela plunged down the valley wall, there was a prominence from which the whole expanse of the valley could be seen. This is truly a scenic highway. The valley here is a fertile, undulating floor. Good rain this summer has decked it with green and spread all the colors of grain over it—wheat, barley, sorghum, and corn. It is a time of rich harvest. Hut tops appeared just above the tips of the corn, and men were wading into the wheat fields with sickles.

This is Oromo country—the largest people group in Ethiopia, numbering over thirty million and spreading from the border of Somalia through central and south Ethiopia, and even down into northern Kenya. They are predominantly Muslim, but Christ has set his love on these people. He has raised up men, transformed and driven by the gospel, to take good news to their people, and there has been rapid advance of the kingdom among them. There are now about seven million Oromo believers—one of them is my friend Michael. He has a great burden that his people would have the Bible in their heart language. There is an Oromo Bible, and there is a high literacy rate among the Oromo people, but the problem is supply. Michael estimates that only 2 percent of Oromo believers have the Scripture in their language. With great effort he was able to secure a few boxes of Oromo New Testaments, and we set out today to make the first delivery to the village of Bosha.

With every turn our road got narrower, as we cut through fields of grain and beneath ancient acacias and "umbrella" trees. The road became a trail, and the trail became a path—until it all ended in a huddle of huts called Bosha. A donkey was nearby; we borrowed him to carry the box of Oromo New Testaments. I thought of the passage in Matthew's Gospel when on Palm Sunday the Lord sent the disciples to "borrow" a donkey: "If anyone says anything to you, you shall say, 'The Lord needs [it],' and he will send [it] at once" (Matt. 21:3). That blessed donkey carried the living Word; ours today carried the written Word.

We wended our way through the fields of Bosha and reached a simple mud-daubed church, where we delivered the Oromo New Testaments. It was stunning to know that just two years ago, the man who now gave out the Scriptures with great delight was the sheikh in this Muslim village, and a fierce persecutor. Sheikh Jaru's two sons had become Christians. When Abdullah and Muzemir testified of their faith in Jesus Christ, their father flew into a rage, beat them with a horsewhip, and kicked them out. For months afterward they endured threats, hunger, and rejection, but they also prayed—boldly—for their dad's salvation and for the other Muslims in Bosha. When newborn Christians can face such persecution, they demonstrate that conversion is not a mental thing—it is a radical, inside-out work of God that is made to last! Through his sons' bold witness and by reading the Scriptures, after a year the sheikh believed and in joyful adoration declared that Jesus, *Isa Masih*, was his Lord! After Jaru's conversion (or as he puts it, after he "became a new person"), he went to the mosque and proclaimed Christ and, as is often the case with the gospel, stirred up both anger and wonder.

Borrowing a donkey

We joined together in a time of praise and prayer of thanksgiving for the gift of the Word. At first I noticed the singing was a bit tempered, a bit reserved. Michael mentioned to me that they were singing in Amharic, the national language which is not their mother tongue. After dispensing with that formality, they sang in Oromo of the power of Jesus to save and for the blessing of receiving his Word for the first time—to read, to hear Jesus speaking Oromo. They sang in their native tongue in joyful worship. It was very lively—but who could blame them? They've seen the iron bars of Islam snapped like a stick. They were dead but have now been raised up by the living Christ. As Isaiah said, "Behold, your God . . . He will come and save you. . . . The eyes of the blind shall be opened, and the ears of the deaf unstopped; then shall the lame man leap like a deer, and the tongue of the mute sing for joy" (Isa. 35:4–6).

Afterward we said our farewells, leaving our newly found brothers and sisters now armed with at least a few copies of the Scriptures in Oromo. The Word and their witness are moving the boundaries of Christ's kingdom outward into more and more Muslim hearts, further shaking the gates of hell here.

The road out took us through fields laden with grain. One family and their cattle were threshing wheat on a wind-swept hilltop, as it has been done here for centuries. Michael took the opportunity, as we passed, to direct a young Muslim named Sultan to the church in Bosha, for the harvest here *is* plenteous.

ZIWAY, ETHIOPIA

Reached Lake Ziway, one of deep lakes in the heart of the valley. It's a magnet for wildlife. Ziway is bursting with birds of every kind. Treaded my way out on a jetty and found flotillas of pelicans, as well as eagles, kingfishers, cormorants, and what must surely be the ugliest bird in the world, the marabou. Their bald heads have red cracks on them and a bit of wiry hair. A pouch hangs down from their ridiculously large beaks, where they keep various bits of rotting fish. The marabou looks like a mistake, a fowl Frankenstein. Poor marabou—only his equally ugly mother could love such a face. I tried to catch one, but he played hard to get.

Before sunset, took a boat out on Lake Ziway in search of hippos. It's surprising that the large, lumpy hippopotamus is actually one of the most dangerous animals in the world, killing more people each year than lions or tigers. But Ziway is a good place to find them in their element, so we went poking around their lairs during their suppertime, hoping to find someone at home. However, hippos that aren't in a zoo are *most* uncooperative! After our first sighting of a pair, we went in for a closer look. The boatman called them up by beating on the bow. I'm not sure what it accomplishes—maybe it annoys them out of the water. We got really close to one—his head glistening in the slanting light before slipping beneath us.

Afterward met up by the lake with Pastor Mekonnen and with Negussi, an Oromo missionary. I have immense respect for these brothers of mine. Over coffee we talked about the progress of the work. Islam has lost so much ground here that there has been a violent reaction in a province to the west, where thirty thousand Muslims have become Christians in the past eight years. In a recent backlash, churches were burned and Christians attacked with machetes. Now the Saudis and even Iranians are broadcasting their hate into the country and building more mosques to stake their claim on Ethiopia. The biggest need to further advance and strengthen the church here is the Scripture in the people's language.

Tomorrow we set out for the villages with our little supply of Oromo Bibles, but I feel a bit like the disciple Andrew standing by the Sea of Galilee with the hungry multitude: "There is a boy here who has five barley loaves and two fish, but what are they for so many?" (John 6:9).

ZIWAY, ETHIOPIA

Gradually the farther shore appears, as the sun chases the moon away. First light skips like bright stones on the waves of Ziway. Birds are making wake-up calls and setting off in search of breakfast. The scene is one that only God can paint. Every color is now before me as the lake reflects the rising day. A path of light scatters the darkness—but I've seen an even greater light here as we've taken the Scriptures deep into Oromo country and met brothers and sisters whose faces shine with gospel glory.

Two days ago Pastor Mekonnen and I, with our remaining supply of Oromo Scriptures, set out for churches and preaching points scattered around Ziway. At Hatay we met an old woman named Arro-kulano, who had for years been a sorceress until she heard the gospel and abandoned the service of demons. In anger over her faith, her Muslim son burned her house down! But the change in his mother's life and the way the Christians loved her and rebuilt her house softened his heart—and the power of the cross did the rest. He gathered with us to praise the Lord Jesus as we sat beneath trees thick with the nests of weaver birds. The songbirds seemed to join in as we lifted our voices and hands in praise.

Mekonnen preached, and a young evangelist named Gulilat interpreted in Oromo. Gulilat is one of a new breed of Ethiopian church planters who go village to village as community development workers. They help improve crop yields or village sanitation, along with witnessing. In other words, they dig latrines in order to make disciples. I asked him which Muslim villages they target. "All of them," Gulilat said matter-of-factly. "We don't skip."

I also met Allam, a woman who walks these roads and loves to share Christ. She was particularly eager to receive a few Oromo New Testaments to share with the women in her group. Afterward, we were refreshed with roasted corn before going deep into the Oromo backcountry.

Yesterday we set out for Malka-buta. Since it was a weekday and harvesttime, only a quarter of the congregation was able to gather. Nevertheless, the children greeted us with song, and there was much joy over the Oromo Scriptures. The congregation here numbers nearly four hundred, but they have no more than a couple dozen Bibles among them. We gave them what we could, and afterward we celebrated a kind of Communion—a fellowship with bread and Coca-Cola to mark this special day. Then we immediately set out for Koticha, a church planted by the Malka-buta church. In fact, the prolific Malka-buta believers "love to tell the story," as the old hymn goes.[1] In the past ten years, they have established nineteen churches and forty-five preaching points. Good news travels fast! The drive was through beautiful country with bad roads. The road got so narrow at one point, it was like driving down a row of corn.

Finally reached Koticha with our ever-dwindling Oromo Scriptures. Above the door of the church a hand-lettered sign proclaimed,

"Jesus Saves!" A Muslim herdsman came in to see what was happening, and Negussi shared how Jesus could save him, too.

Our fellowship around the Word continued around the table, as the Christians shared a meal with us. Afterward, they even shared their mules so we could reach a village called Chirri, the farthest point that the gospel has penetrated thus far. We had only five Oromo New Testaments left. So few. This is indeed precious Seed.

Our animals were sure-footed and well acquainted with the ups and downs of this remote hill country. It was a perfect day for such happy work—our yoke was easy and our burden light. When we reached the village, there was much joy over the Bibles, and the people sang,

> I witness of the One who died for me.
> I witness of the One who rose again.
> I witness of the One who gave me new life.

Their witness is of the life-and-death difference that Jesus makes. It is their answer to his great invitation: "I am the bread of life; whoever comes to me shall not hunger, . . . whoever comes to me I will never cast out" (John 6:35, 37). As we rode on, my heart echoed their gospel joy, still amazed that Christ asked me to come, too.

JUBA, SOUTH SUDAN

Another flight. Took a prop plane from Addis to Juba, the capital of the world's newest nation—South Sudan. I tagged along with Michael, who is here to replicate what he and his team are doing in Ethiopia—developing self-sustaining ministries for both church planting and the care of orphans. Both tasks seem as vast and uncharted as this new country.

The flight took us across hundreds of miles of green wilderness. I didn't see a single road until we neared Juba. Because there is little access to much of South Sudan, some places aren't even on the map, and the number of people is unknown. The population is only wildly guessed at as being between eight and fourteen million people. Whatever the numbers, the war that gave birth to the nation has a more accurate but grim census: two million dead; four million displaced. The killing was on the scale of a world war, but within an area the size of Texas. Sudan's civil war was launched by the Muslim north against the historically Christian population in the southern region. In addition, rival tribes and militias added their toll to the killing fields. The northern capital of Khartoum was the center of an effort to subjugate and Islamicize all of Sudan, and radical Muslims from other countries also joined in. Even Osama bin Laden was invited to Khartoum to set up shop. It was here in Sudan that the mastermind of al-Qaeda cut his teeth on killing. His friends said his years in Khartoum were among the happiest of his life.[2] The South endured twenty years of war before a peace agreement was patched together and independence achieved just four months ago.

On our plane's approach to Juba, we crossed the White Nile, which flows up from Uganda and divides the capital. It's exciting to set foot in a new country—all the more to set foot in the newest country. Here the nation's birthday celebration is still a fresh memory, but the party is already over. If South Sudan is the Wild West of Africa, then Juba is one big, sprawling, dusty frontier town. I have read that there are at present only sixty-seven miles of paved roads in all of South Sudan—half of those being around the homes and offices of government leaders in Juba. I guess we were traveling in the wrong neighborhood!

Juba is a magnet for people as poor as the roads, but the lack of jobs, set against the flood of desperate Sudanese, has resulted in a 90 percent unemployment rate in the city. For a generation, farming and fighting were the primary occupations, and so there is little infrastructure or industry here. The industry I did come across was heartbreaking. Along the roads families of rock-breakers were making gravel by hand and hammer. It seemed to me a miniature of this new country—a people with hard-fought, hard-won freedom now struggling with the hard work of keeping it.

Sat by the Nile yesterday morning beneath a huge mango tree and listened in on Michael and Kebede, his right-hand man, talking ministry strategy with several Sudanese pastors. Kebede is Oromo; he is intense, encyclopedic, and his administrative skills are as sharp and varied as a Swiss Army knife. What is impressive to me is the caliber of leadership among these Ethiopians. What they are doing in their country, as well as here in South Sudan, is nation-shaking. Training that moves from generation to generation takes work, focus, mentoring, translators, and logistics. Conferences are easy, but multiplying leaders and overcoming lots of geographic and linguistic barriers is not. Here in Sudan they are taking the first steps to equip fifteen hundred church planters, who are taking the gospel across South Sudan and into the Arab North.

Set out early this morning for Rejaf, the scene of intense see-saw fighting during the war. Thousands were killed here, and this area is still not clear of mines; but survivors are returning from refugee camps to resettle here nonetheless. A pastor from Juba named Darious agreed to take me out. During the war years, he served as an itinerant evangelist all across hostile northern Sudan, including Darfur and the Nubian Mountains. For him, the war isn't history; like other South Sudanese, it is simply his story. Darious's father and mother and most of his brothers were killed in the bloodletting.

Reached Rejaf midmorning and met Pastor Joseph, who shepherds the flock here. Huts and signs of life are slowly reappearing. Joseph pastors the church and runs the school but receives no salary for any of it. His garden sustains him and his family. Life and ministry are struggles here in a village filled with widows. We walked to the foot of Rejaf, a little mountain, a striking heap of boulders ascending above the savannah. The hike was like swimming through a sea of grass. Apart from poisonous snakes and the fact that no one was sure all the mines have been cleared, this would be an awesome place for hide-and-seek.

Below Rejaf, we came across an old cemetery where British soldiers and the first missionaries to come to southern Sudan are buried. More than a century ago, men and women brought the gospel up the Nile and made Rejaf a center for Christianity. This explains one of the reasons that Muslims fighting for Khartoum burned all the churches and homes here, for Rejaf was both strategic high ground and Christian symbol. Here British soldiers and missionaries sleep far from home beneath the briars and savannah grass. I thought of the lines of Rupert Brooke's old elegy, *The Soldier.*

> If I should die, think only this of me:
> That there's some corner of a foreign field
> That is for ever England.[3]

Birds and the nearby Nile sing over their graves and over fields where blood still cries out from the ground.

Afterward visited Pastor Joseph's school. The school building was constructed a hundred years ago by missionaries but was destroyed along with the rest of Rejaf during the war. For awhile it was used for barracks, but then was abandoned. Since it is a seven-mile walk to the nearest school, Joseph took matters into his own hands. He patched bullet holes, organized volunteer teachers, and opened the broken doors to one hundred children. Goats bed down in the classrooms at night, so a teacher's first duty is to sweep up the goat dung each morning.

In addition to the three Rs, the students are studying English, learning it in part from a Christian primer. Prior to the South's breaking away from the Muslim North, the masters in Khartoum forced Christian children here to study Arabic and the Koran. This South Sudanese version of a McGuffey reader is as clear a sign of the nation's independence as is their new flag. Signs of hope for the new nation are few and far between, but I found one today in the shadow of Rejaf. The children are beautiful, and the school brings life to a place that has seen so much death. Their singing and laughter has turned a battleground into a playground.

Pastor Joseph's school

The sun is drawing down. Found a quiet refuge along the Nile, a place to write and watch the river and the day slip by. Boys are swimming in the surf and casting nets for their supper. A flock of birds hurry along this shimmering avenue, looking for a place to bed down. The Nile flows northward on its long march, past Khartoum, past the pyramids and Cairo, and on to the Mediterranean. It's a path I shall soon take, too.

CAIRO, EGYPT

Met up with Michele yesterday. She is a human rights lawyer and brave sister in Christ who is here gathering evidence and testimonies of Christian persecution. There is no shortage of work. We were in the trenches together in Pakistan, and so it is good to team up again. Late last night at a safe house we met one couple on the run because the wife has become a Christian and her dad and mom would like to kill her. Also met a Coptic Christian named Athanasius, who brought video evidence of torture and church burnings.

Today traveled with an Egyptian pastor named Jonah to the garbage city of El Khma in Cairo. Tens of thousands of people live in several such "cities" in Cairo. Here, the desperately poor and desperately hungry live, picking through mountains of garbage, looking for something to sell or something to eat. A few roads and footpaths cut between the rotting heaps and the pitiful shelters where the garbage-pickers live. It rained last night, turning our path into a slurry of mud, raw sewage, and dead rats. The hot, Egyptian sun drew off steam and stench, which hung thick in the air. Down every dark alley and near every hovel, I saw women digging through huge sacks of garbage; and kids, accustomed to one meal a day, were licking food wrappers to get some taste of food. Some of the children have bites on their hands and faces left by pigs with which they have struggled for food.

Jonah took us to visit one of the families he ministers to. Eight children and their mother live in a room about ten-by-ten feet. At the gate, a donkey that had carried garbage all of his miserable life lay bloated and rotting in the sun. Jonah gathered all the children and the mama together, and they reviewed some memory verses. Then he told the story of the woman at the well and about Christ, the Water of Life. Jonah serves as Christ's hands in this place. He is not just popping in with a few Bible stories, though. He is also teaching them a trade so they can escape this place, and he is counseling them, loving them, and leading them to the Lord. He said when he first came to El Khma that he didn't think he could do this. It was overwhelming. There is a level of need here that is utterly beyond his ability to meet, but that is where God comes in. Perhaps that is why Jonah taught these kids to memorize Philippians 4:13, which they enthusiastically quoted for us: "I can do all things through him [Christ] who strengthens me."

They were old when Abraham, Joseph, and Moses were here.

GIZA, EGYPT

We were hardly across the Nile before the pyramids could be seen, rising above the sprawling jumble of apartments bristling with satellite dishes and dusty, faded billboards advertising Pepsi and Pizza Hut in Arabic. It is a testimony to their grandeur that the great pyramids remain imposing, even above the modern clutter. There is an awesome indifference to time here. The pyramids were old when Abraham, Joseph, and Moses walked here, and though nearly fifty centuries have swept over them, they are still amazing. As we were out exploring these ancient wonders, a solar eclipse occurred. A veil fell over the plateau, covering the pyramids in a strange light without shadows. It reminded me of one of the plagues during the time of Moses, like a live, eerie chapter out of Exodus!

Of course, I had to do the tourist thing, so I took a good, bucking camel ride about the pyramids. The dromedary camel gives a loftier, leggier ride than the Bactrian camels I have ridden in China. The Bactrian is more like riding a horse, since the saddle is between the two humps; whereas with the dromedary, the rider is perched on top of the single hump. "Why did the Lord make two kinds of camels?" That is the riddle I posed to the Sphinx.

ON THE RAIL FROM LUXOR TO ASYUT, EGYPT

Yesterday checked out of our hotel in Maadi at three in the morning and caught an early flight from Cairo to Luxor, which is ancient Thebes. We spent the day exploring the Valley of the Kings, home to the pharoahs' splendid tombs, cryptic crypts chiseled deep into the white stone mountains, which glisten in blinding brilliance beneath the rays of "Ra."

The temple of Hatshepsut was quite impressive with its carved walls recalling great campaigns in Cush and the underworld. Then there was the Luxor Temple with its massive colonnades and lotus-like capitals. How is it that the splendor and the sheer genius of ancient Egypt bears no resemblance to the Egypt of today?

I was reminded of that this morning as we took a taxi to the train station early, going along streets in Luxor where no doubt Joseph once road his chariot in splendor. Today, though, the glory has definitely departed. Crumbling mud-brick cafes huddle along broken streets where men with languid eyes and leathery faces sit smoking *sheesha* and sipping tea out of grimy glasses.

Now we are off to Asyut, a five-hour train trip from Luxor. There we will visit the Christian orphanage run by George, or *Baba George*, as he is known by his large family of nearly four hundred orphans. The place is an oasis of light and hope—square in the middle of a stronghold of Islam, the birthplace of the Muslim Brotherhood. It will be good to spend a few days with the children and see what God has sustained.

My train window is like a picture frame in motion—long, warm rays sift through the fine dust that stirs over the plain and the palm groves. At times the train skirts within a stone's throw of the Nile, and then it turns back into the valley where snowy-white egrets stalk about the green fields, resembling littered laundry drying in the sun.

Our train slows through little, mud-brick towns along the way. At rail crossings, local traffic stands and stares. It is a jam of donkeys and dusty carts, grinning boys gnawing on sticks of raw cane, old men with furrowed faces and immaculately white turbans and beards to match, and black-draped women, peering out of the slit in their burkas—their veils swept by our motion.

ON THE RAIL TO CAIRO, EGYPT

The sun slips swiftly beyond the Nile as our Cairo-bound train rumbles on. It's my last night in Egypt. For now, though, it is time to scribble a few notes about the day.

Awoke this morning to the sound of birds and children singing. The orphans were practicing some choir numbers in the courtyard. It was joyful praise in contrast to the surround sound of the Muslim call to prayer, blaring from a dozen loudspeakers from mosques that encircle the orphanage.

At the gates of the orphanage near the chapel, extra soldiers took up their stations, for this is the Lord's Day. Because of the grenade bombings of churches by Muslim terrorists and the murder of Christians (some as young as four years old), the government provides extra security as a precaution against the more zealous members of this "religion of peace." To me, it's no small irony that Asyut in the time of the pharaohs was called Lycopolis, which means "City of Wolves."

The service was a blessed time, especially when the kindergarten choir sang, "Jesus Loves Me." Michele shared her testimony, and I preached on God's precious promise in Isaiah 41: "Fear not, for I am with you; . . . I will help you, I will uphold you" (Isa. 41:10).

Baba George told me this morning that some of his church members sleep at the church. These Muslim converts cannot go home or they will be killed; so they work during the day and sleep at the church at night. It is their refuge. Despite the dangers in evangelizing, they have first-century courage, as it was said of Peter and John in Acts 4: "When they saw the boldness . . . they recognized that they had been with Jesus" (Acts 4:13). The pastor told me, "Some say to me, 'Keep a low profile,' but what does that do? The Christian life is full of risks."

Baba George

Afterward we ventured outside the orphanage compound to see a few sights. On the outskirts of Asyut, armed guards accompanied us for protection from possible attacks. Even when we got out of the car, four or five men with pistols and AK-47s walked with us. After a while, our Muslim "muscle" softened up their tough-guy image with us, and we were chatting together in broken Arabic and English and picking apples.

Visited the Christian cemetery beneath the cave-riddled mountains near Asyut, where an old tradition has it that Joseph, Mary, and the baby Jesus stayed after fleeing Herod's henchmen. In a neglected corner of the cemetery lie many missionaries who brought the gospel to Egypt nearly a century ago and died far from home. The desert heat shimmered over a scattering of crumbling, mud-brick markers and broken epitaphs. It was so desolate. I thought of how these men and women, when they set out for the field, must have parted from their families with kisses and tears, but also with the joy that rushes the heart when Jesus is near. They crossed the Atlantic to tell people about their Friend and Savior. They now rest here, their lives poured out like water on this parched ground. They crossed an ocean—but never recrossed it. For them, missionary service was a one-way ticket. Of course, cross-bearing is a one-way ticket, too.

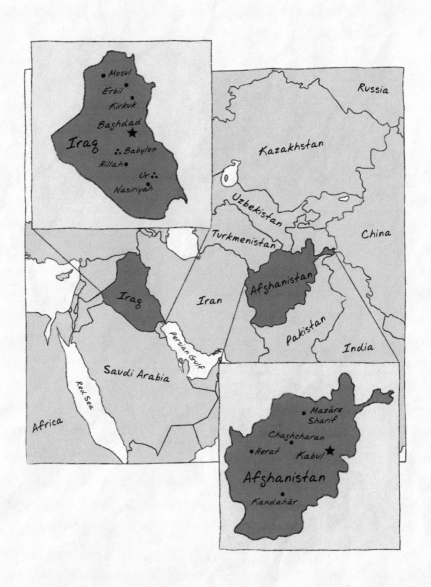

8

DIMMED BY DUST

Afghanistan and Iraq

Sandstorm in the Hazarajat

Samuel Zwemer, the leading voice for missions to the unreached Islamic world, wrote in *The Glory of the Impossible*, "Is Afghanistan sealed against the entrance of the Christian missionary? Or is the land only waiting for those who will pay the price of bursting its barriers?"[1]

A century after Zwemer, Afghanistan remains one of the most intractable pieces of the 10/40 puzzle. The latest wave of gospel work followed the United States and NATO fight to free the country of the control of the Taliban and its al-Qaeda clients, some of whom carried out the September 11th attacks on the United States. Fighting a borderless war with an elusive enemy over a long campaign,

NATO forces have encountered bitter winters, blistering summers, and harsh terrain laced with a patchwork of tribes that are both divided and united by ancient hatreds. Their courage and sacrifice are exemplary, and many have laid down their lives in the cause of freedom. All of this, too, can be said for the first-wave forces of Christians serving in Afghanistan and Iraq. Their long campaign has also been marked by struggle, suffering, and untimely graves. Yet there have also been victories. Did Christ not promise this? For he said that not even the gates of hell—not even the gates of Islam— would be able to withstand the advance of his kingdom! Gospel outposts here are small and scattered and born into the fellowship of Christ's sufferings—like the six Afghan men I know who meet on a different day and at a different time each week to avoid detection. Or the woman in a burka who received a New Testament and after two years invited the missionary to her home and introduced other family members who had received Christ. Holding up the Book, she said, "This is the truth we have been seeking for years." So the kingdom choir continues to gather, even in impossible places, for the Lamb is worthy!

ATLANTA, GEORGIA

Bound for Afghanistan with Beth and Jenni—friends, sisters, nurses. As our plane prepares to board, scores of American soldiers wait for flights to the Middle East. I recognize their destinations, whether Iraq or Afghanistan, by the patches on their crisp, desert camos. It's a quiet gate—their thoughts are their own as they wait. Some fidget with their backpacks, iPods, or even a new wedding band. They face a long and uncertain winter of fighting, but before that, a long flight and more waiting.

We have our own campaign to wage in Afghanistan—not with guns and armor, "for the weapons of our warfare are not of the flesh but have divine power to destroy strongholds" (2 Cor. 10:4). It's a fourteen-hour flight to the eastern edge of Arabia. From there, it's another fourteen hours before reaching Afghanistan.

They are calling our flight. Soldiers are hoisting their packs on, and I am restless and ready.

KABUL, AFGHANISTAN

Arrived in Kabul this morning. Flying from India with its broad, checkered plains, there was no question when we crossed into Afghanistan, as the Hindu Kush reached up to us like a tidal wave in stone. My first impression of Kabul from the air was of a city in a sandbox. On the ground, the streets swirl with dust, big turbans, black beards, blue burkas, troops, and lots of guns.

There is much to write, but for now, sleep beckons me. The sky over Kabul glows in warm colors beneath the descent of night. The dusty orange haze is specked with kites and Army helicopters. The call to prayer, the *azan*, sounds in the distance, calling Mohammed's followers to fall on their faces.

JALALABAD, AFGHANISTAN

Set out this morning with Beth and her coworker Cheryl, who has ministered here for four years. Reached Jalalabad after a tense drive along a stretch of road popular with suicide bombers. Afghan Army and regional police were everywhere, setting up random checkpoints. Smaller but beefier NATO units supplemented the local security forces. After the gauntlet, we reached the city by early afternoon. Along the way, we saw a clan of Kuchi nomads spread out over a barren stretch of sand along the road, where they had pitched their tents that were like those Abraham, Isaac, and Jacob lived in. Herds of black goats dotted the wasteland, and camels lolled about the settlement.

We enjoyed a wonderful meal from a Pashtun believer, a secret disciple named Mohammed. Pashtun hospitality is legendary, and so is purdah—the division between men and women. The only indication of the presence of a woman in the house was the steady stream of fine dishes that filled the floor as we reclined around the wall on *toshaks*. Mohammed's sons washed our hands in a basin and brought in platters of *kabuli pilau, mantu* dumplings, and grilled mutton sausage called *chapli kebabs*. We finished off with grapes and tea spiced with cardamom. Mohammed showed us great courtesy, and the joy he had in giving it was the very definition of hospitality. He was trained as an engineer by Russians during the Soviet occupation, and so he gave us one of their proverbs as we drank our last cup and were thanking him for the fine meal. He said, "It's not what you eat that's important, but who you eat it with."

Kabul, Afghanistan

Mohammed's daughter came in for a time to join her young brothers. She is a beautiful girl with eyes that are deep and calm, and her father shows great affection for her. As we left the house, I had a fleeting glimpse of the other lady of the house—a translucent curtain screened a veiled woman, half-hidden as she peered around the doorpost at her guests. The men went out so Beth and Cheryl could stay and greet Mrs. Mohammed. Beth said afterward that Mrs. Mohammed is a beautiful woman with the same deep calm eyes as her daughter.

While I waited for the ladies, Mohammed plucked a most fragrant rose from his garden and gave it to me. I've never had a man give me a rose before—but it's OK this time, for it is a Pashtun custom of honor. And so, as we drove back down the Jalalabad Road through the gauntlet of guns, the contrast of war and roses was a fragrant irony of life in Afghanistan.

KABUL, AFGHANISTAN

As the sun sinks over Kabul, a muezzin chants out the *azan* from a nearby mosque. Its cant seems especially piercing and disgusting to me, like the cackle of a demon. Blood calls out from the ground, for this morning Gayle Williams was gunned down by the Taliban just a few streets away. She had been here for about a year working with the poor who have been disabled by landmines. As a physical therapist, she had been the hands of Christ to many in Kandahar, but the killings and kidnappings there had brought her to Kabul. She was shot as she walked to work in Kart-e-Char.

We went over to the elementary school right away to watch the children of the Christian workers while they sorted things out to implement a lockdown, since it is evident that foreign aid workers are being targeted for assassination. The last time we were together with Gayle and the other believers, we were all worshipping together. Today we were sorrowing together.

The Taliban claimed "credit" for the killing, charging Gayle guilty of the crime of "spreading Christianity." And so she joins Stephen's ranks—those "of whom the world was not worthy" (Heb. 11:38). Now Gayle stands in light, her wounds healed by wounded hands, and she's safe, comforted, and home. That's how it looks on the other side of the thin line of life. On this side, though, there are questions, sorrow, and blood on a back street in Kabul.

* * *

We've been in lockdown at the guesthouse for several days now. Only essential travel is permitted for now. The lockdown is frustrating, but we make the best of it. It's a time for travelers to sit around the table and trade stories, whether of off-roading in Mongolia or comparing Kirgiz naan with the bread that comes from Afghan ovens. We get a landmine tutorial, learn the best motorcycle route across the Sahara, and hear about the legends of Chugwater, Wyoming. It's eclectic, encyclopedic, and sometimes exciting, as when my roommate Ian told of surviving a climb in the snowy Himalayas, clinging to life on the icy fringe of death.

In quiet places here, among trusted friends, we also share kingdom stories. Ian told me of when he was working in Meymana, a Talib-infiltrated area in the Turkestan Range. The local mullah was angry with him and wanted to denounce him as a *kafir* (infidel) before the village elders at the evening meal. The situation was explosive. In front of them all, the mullah asked Ian, "Why do you call the prophet *Isa* [Jesus] the Messiah?" With all eyes on him, Ian was granted boldness and words to speak. He first established that Isa is "our prophet"—one we share, since he is called a prophet in the Koran. The mullah agreed. Then Ian explained the deeper meaning of *Masih* (Messiah). More than a title, it means "to touch, to heal"—"the touch that heals." Only Jesus Christ had power to heal. Even the Koran acknowledges this. For these men it was like sweeping sand off an ancient oracle: Isa is the Messiah! The room erupted in spontaneous joy, and the mullah fell silent. Oh, the power of truth!

Yes, this lockdown is frustrating, but this is the way it is with first-wave forces—sometimes you're flat on your face just staying alive, sometimes you run forward, but most often you crawl, looking for a break in the wall. Retreat is not an option. That was evident in our worship service held at a nearby house this morning. Despite Gayle's murder this week and all the subsequent threats, the main prayer request was "pray that our agencies back home won't make us leave."

The gathering was a tender time, too, remembering Gayle's Christlike life—Christlike to the end. It seems the Lord was preparing her for home because after the kidnapping of a coworker two months ago, she told a friend that, though shaken, she was prepared to die in Afghanistan. Tomorrow she will be buried here, and so another cross is raised in this place—a kingdom stake driven into this barren land by the indisputable power of Calvary love. Even the gates of hell creak and shudder and will be crushed by the force of it.

Nate closed our worship in an unusual way by reading a poem by Baranczak entitled *If China*. A ten-year veteran of Afghanistan, he read it with tears. I learned afterward that five years ago, when he and his family had to flee Kandahar for their lives, they lost everything they owned. One of the things was Nate's guitar, which had given him much joy over the years. He hasn't played since—it must seem too painful to take it back off the altar.

> If china, then only the kind
> you wouldn't miss under the movers' shoes
>   or the treads of a tank;
> if a chair, then one that's not too comfortable, or
> you'll regret getting up and leaving;
> if clothes, then only what will fit in one suitcase;
> if books, then those you know by heart;
> if plans, then the ones you can give up
> when it comes time for the next move,
> to another street, another continent or epoch
> or world.
> Who told you to settle in?
> Who told you this or that would last forever?
> Didn't anyone ever tell you that you'll never
> in the world
> feel at home here?[2]

Two more foreigners were shot today in a Taliban-style killing. Kabul is turning into a hornet's nest. I'm glad we're headed to the western Hazarajat tomorrow to visit the workers and see the opportunities there. It is a high, remote region over 150 miles from here, but the twenty-hour road trip is too risky because of the Taliban, so we will fly as far as we can and then take a back road the rest of the way to Chaghcharan. One good thing about getting out of Kabul is that the Hazarajat region is virtually free of landmines, so at least we'll be able to get out and walk again.

CHAGHCHARAN, AFGHANISTAN

Late morning took a flight from Kabul to Yakawlang by way of Bamiyan. The eight-seater prop skirted over the barren Baba Mountains, reaching a dirt strip in Bamiyan about noon. The runway was marked by a crashed plane on one end and a hand-lettered sign welcoming visitors to the Silk Road Hotel on the other end. Actually, pilgrims, traders, and invaders as far back as Alexander the Great have passed through here. For at least fifteen centuries, travelers along the Silk Road here were greeted by two huge standing Buddhas carved in massive niches along the canyon road walls. The Taliban blew the "idols" up several years ago, leaving only the giant keyhole caves that housed them. These gaping holes are today's monuments—a fitting tribute to the violence and emptiness of radical Islam.

Departed Bamiyan and soon arrived in Yakawlang. Despite the remoteness of it, the local police chief arrived to detain us and harass the pilot for landing without his permission. He fumed that no one in Kabul informed him. "We have laws out here!" he declared, gesturing out over a wasteland checkered with a few mud-brick dwellings. The chief's delegation included a donkey, a few curious shepherd boys who stood staring, and a Barney Fife–like deputy bearing an ancient Kalashnikov, which was the only *real* law as far as I could see.

After delaying us for an hour, the chief finally allowed us to continue. Took the remote road through the Sar Jangal, avoiding the riskier road toward Panjao. Our road was more of a dirt path of dust beaten to talcum, which plunged down embankments without warning. At other times it toed the steep mountains along the Tungul Pass like a tightrope act. Ever changing, the Sar Jangal road was at times a riverbed, which we shared with women beating out their laundry on rocks along the rivulet. Beyond it, the high country often resembled the moon, only with a sky so intensely blue it hurt to look at it.

Passed a village where a *buz-kashi* was underway—a rarity for a foreigner to see. About twenty horsemen on two teams were competing for a headless goat, which they skillfully fought each other for—kind of like football on horseback.

Our stops were few because night travel can be dangerous even here, but feeling famished and having had little to eat all day, we stopped in a village called Da Mardod. The women were fair-skinned and not veiled, and their children were clothed in bright, dusty silks. These are the Hazara—all bearing the features of their Mongolian ancestors who first arrived here on horseback with Genghis Khan. Other than curious smiles and a disgusting latrine, the village had few amenities. Hussein, our driver, managed to find some food—packets of Iranian cookies. We wolfed them down, but I broke a tooth on one from a stone in the flour.

Pressed on, conscious of the approaching night. As the sun slipped beyond the range, the amber hills turned to amethyst. In the last light, Hussein suddenly pulled over, and he and a companion got out to pray toward Mecca. They spread their *desmals* out for a prayer rug and ritually washed their hands and faces in the fine dust since water could not be had. After they finished their routine and snapped the dust out of their cloaks, we proceeded on, reaching Chaghcharan this evening. Haven't seen any of the town yet because the only night light here is starlight, which is breathtaking since we are ten thousand feet up with no electricity. The night canopy is so full of stars that it seems ready to fall beneath the weight of its glory. Before settling in for the night, our traveling companion Marja pointed out where our road continued. She said, "This is the way to Herat, toward Iran. Take this road and you will reach Herat in two days." However, my first thought was that since the Taliban control the road, I would likely reach heaven before I reach Herat. No, I think we have traveled enough for one day!

CHAGHCHARAN, AFGHANISTAN

Woke up this morning with an abscessed finger. Set out after breakfast with Dr. Ben, a Christian surgeon here, to get it fixed. The walk down "Main Street" of Chaghcharan gave me a chance to see what I couldn't see last night—smoke coiled over an assortment of mud-brick shops straddling a dusty road with a few side streets squeezing in between them. Beyond the little cluster of brown boxes are brown mountains etched with brown trails and a spattering of brown goats. The air was sharp, and I noticed men, mindful of the approaching winter, fashioning stovepipes out of coffee cans. Another man was measuring out grain with stone weights. Old men with white beards and silk turbans sat along the roadside fingering their prayer beads. Stopped at the naan shop—the flat bread was stacked high. Naan is a staple at every Afghan meal, and so we crowded in with others to buy our daily bread.

Ben and I then walked on to the hospital—a mud-brick compound that serves the entire district of three hundred and fifty thousand people in the rugged Hazarajat. The sick were already gathering for the day, so the gate was crowded and the "parking lot" filled with donkeys. Went into the OR, where Ben lanced my finger with a razor. The cleaning lady worked around us, sweeping up dust and bloody bandages from the floor. The hospital is dark, dirty, and primitive; yet, considering there is no indoor plumbing, no refrigeration, electricity only from solar panels and a weak generator, and a largely illiterate staff, I think they are doing extraordinary work.

Tonight we gathered for worship at Ben's house. We all huddled around the *bukharia*, the kerosene stove, and sang hymns. I preached from Genesis 15, where the Lord took Abram outside and showed him stars as breathtaking as those here in Chaghcharan. He told Abram, as it were, "I made all these stars. Don't you think I can make a child?" "And he believed the LORD, and he counted it to him for righteousness" (Gen. 15:6). This is the God who also could say to Abram, "Fear not," and he says the same to us, despite the Taliban.

It was a blessing to preach and to fellowship with brothers and sisters here. There were fourteen of us huddled around the stove. These gospel workers—doctors, nurses, community specialists—are the first-wave forces of the kingdom's advance. And it *is* going forward, even in the heart of Afghanistan. Despite the great risk, there are several men in this town who have received Christ as well as women who have taken Bibles and slipped them beneath their veils. At the close, we sang "Knowing You." It's a beautiful description of Philippians 3:10 and a powerful testimony of those who have taken up their cross and followed Christ to the very heart of Afghanistan.

> Now my heart's desire is to know you more,
> To be found in you and known as yours.
> To possess by faith what I could not earn,
> All surpassing gift of righteousness.
> Oh, to know the power of your risen life,
> And to know you in your sufferings.
> To become like you in your death, my Lord,
> So with you to live and never die.[3]

KHORZARI, AFGHANISTAN

I am sitting in the village mosque waiting for the elders to assemble to talk over the community development work here. The simple mud-brick mosque clings to a mountainside along the footpath leading to Khorzari. Two logs prop up the roof of mud-daubed branches. An old man sits before me propped up against one of the logs. He has a gray-peppered beard and a brown-striped *lunggi* wrapped around his head and tied up about his weathered face to ward off the cold. He is studying me as I write and sketch him.

Above him is a portrait of the Ayatollah Khomeini scowling down upon us. I am propped next to the window, which is open to the valley. A light snow drifts in and disappears into the worn red carpet. Tea has arrived—time to talk.

* * *

Tonight I am beneath a single naked bulb suspended from a wire. My eyes strain to read by the fading light. The solar panels, too, are strained to near exhaustion from days of wintry skies, which drape the valley of Hari Rud. A heavy snow is falling right now, and I am praying for passable roads to reach Yakawlang on Monday and then a flight to Kabul. The thought of being delayed here indefinitely is too difficult to consider right now. Cold creeps into this room, and my eyes hurt.

CHAGHCHARAN, AFGHANISTAN

Our last day in Chaghcharan. Beth spent the morning making rounds at the hospital. It looks like baby Tahira may live. She should be able to go home soon—once her mother finds a donkey to take them there. Tahira is a seven-month-old girl who weighs just seven pounds. Whether the baby will survive back home is anyone's guess. One mother and four babies have died here already this week. These have become part of the world's worst infant mortality rates. In Afghanistan one out of four children does not live beyond his fifth birthday. Too weak to cry, Tahira's hollow, haunting eyes put a face to such terrible statistics.

Malnutrition claims many children. Leah, a nurse here, related to me yesterday a story of one of her young patients, a two-year-old girl named Nek-Bekhyr. Her name means "fortune," but none has followed her miserable existence. She has experienced only a gnawing hunger that eats up life itself. Leah described how Nek-Bekhyr was so malnourished that her corneas had melted away. Leah pleaded with the mother not to take the girl back home, where she would soon die without care. Leah begged her, "She can live, and in time we can teach her. She can have a life." "What kind of life would a blind girl have?" the mother replied, and she took her daughter back to her village, where no doubt Nek-Bek has already been laid in a narrow hole hacked into this hard land. Leah's eyes brimmed with tears of sorrow to recall this little life that merciless reality had pulled from her arms.

Tahira and her mother

The day is waning. The slanting light flickers in the snowmelt. The *azan* echoes in the streets. I think of Leah's tears over a blind baby as good as dead. In this stronghold of Islam, where are the Iranians with their universities and wealth? Why have they not sent doctors and nurses here? Where are the Saudis, the Egyptians, or the people of the Emirates awash in oil and designer islands? These countries are sending fighters and suicide bombers, but not doctors and nurses. Out here among the poorest and neediest, it is Christians—not Muslims—who are caring for the sick and dying. It is not because we are better than they are. It is because our God is better than their god. Leah, Beth, Jenni, Ben, and others here who, having received grace and mercy, show grace and mercy. The kingdom of Saud is not represented here, but the kingdom of Christ is. His servants have taken up their cross, and by grace they carry it through dim hospital wards and along the snowy mountain paths that now catch the last glint of day.

ON THE ROAD TO THE PANJSHIR

Scratching out a few notes from the back of a truck as we jostle down a dusty road north of Kabul. Ali is our driver, a quiet, kindly man. Despite the twisted arm he has from a war wound, he is a wily maneuverer through the maze of Kabul's streets.

As we make our way out of the city, there is a series of roundabouts on the way toward Mazar. Along these circles, stalls toe the road, spilling over with mounds of watermelons and bright tomatoes, along with racks of gutted goats and sheep flecked with flies. The circles swirl with soldiers, with carters, and with women in grimy burkas, looking like blue ghosts. The veil is Islam's "gift" to women, and the burka is the Afghan "improvement" on the gift. It's the answer to the old proverb here, "A woman's place is in the home or the grave." The burka offers a middle ground of anonymity and nonentity with its head-to-toe covering, allowing only a little mesh at the top in order to see and suck in air in this desert land.

Drove on to Kut with Abdul and Mohammed. In the distance, the imposing Panjshir Range spread over the horizon like a curtain of cracked ice. The men of Kut were working on their road but took a break to smoke and to hear what Abdul had to say. We all sat on an old red carpet spread out along a riverbank and talked. Some of the aged elders were there, too. Their voluminous *lunggis* seemed too big for their shrunken faces, which were weary and furrowed like cracked leather. They extended Afghan hospitality to us and sent two young men out to pick mulberries and sour cherries, which they washed in snowmelt and served in a basket. We all gathered around and gobbled them down.

Afghan hospitality

The obvious leader among the men was Mahfooz, a forty-year-old, former mujahideen commander in this valley. He seemed to take a liking to me, and afterward he invited me to his home. Walking along an old riverbed, he pointed out places where his men died and where they killed many Russian soldiers in the liberation of Kut, but revenge slept in the ground along with the corpses because three years ago Mahfooz's seven-year-old son was killed by an old Soviet landmine on the ridge just above his home.

KABUL, AFGHANISTAN

I woke up this morning to the annoying call to prayer crackling over a loudspeaker from a nearby mosque. I'm sure those things must be a recording on a timer, for who in their right mind would be up and waking everyone else up so early? Actually, it gave me a needed and precious two hours before daybreak of prayer and rejoicing in Jesus—his cross, his love. The lines of one song I listened to were particularly perfect for the moment.

On such love, my soul, still ponder,
Love so great, so rich, so free;
Say, while lost in holy wonder,
"Why, O Lord, such love to me?"
Hallelujah! Grace shall reign![4]

It was a needed reminder, for these are difficult days of threats, searches, imprisonments, and narrow escapes for believers here. The stress and weariness of it all shows on Cheryl's face. Last night we gathered for prayer in a house just around the corner from where Gayle was shot by the Taliban. Her blood still stains the wall where they shot her. After the meeting, they were sorting books to burn so they don't fall into the hands of the police. As the noose of house searches and interrogations tightens, there have been more and more books and papers to burn. I think the birthday present Beth gave me yesterday was one that she spared from the fire. I'm glad for it because neither of us could have stood to see a dear old Samuel Zwemer book go up in flames. Yet Dr. Zwemer would have understood, for he himself wrote over a century ago:

> When you read in reports of troubles and opposition, of burning up books, imprisoning colporteurs, and expelling workers, you must not think that the Gospel is being defeated. It is conquering. What we see under such circumstances is only the dust in the wake of the ploughman. God is turning the world upside down that it may be right side up when Jesus comes. He that plougheth should plough in hope. We may not be able to see a harvest yet in this country, but furrow after furrow, the soil is getting ready for the seed.[5]

That kingdom vision in Revelation, when the ransomed from every tribe and language and nation—and that includes Afghanistan—are gathered in joyful worship in their King's throne room, is a staggering vision. But today, here in the wake of the ploughman, it's a vision dimmed by dust, smoke, and blood-stained walls.

TWO MONTHS LATER, ASHTABULA, OHIO

Bright leaves are hanging on for dear life as an autumn wind tugs at them and tousles the green outfield. A faded scoreboard stares blankly, waiting for another baseball season. Soon it will be capped with snow and fringed with icicles, but for now the sun is absolutely brilliant and it feels like the last day of summer.

Arrived in Ashtabula a bit early and am waiting at this deserted baseball diamond. I have my choice of bleacher seats as I wait for Chris and Joe, pastors over in nearby Madison, where I'll preach tonight. They're delayed a bit, so it gives me time for coffee and a breather after two days on the road.

Ashtabula is the site of the infamous train wreck that claimed the life of the great hymn writer Philip Bliss. I'm too close in my travels not to see it, so that's why I am here. Both Chris and Joe, besides pastoring, are themselves hymn writers and composers—five-talent men who are ever busy about their Master's business. They've agreed to show me the site of the 1876 train disaster. I want to see it, for Bliss has been a blessing to me for as long as I've known how to sing.

I remember when I was no more than five or six. I got up very early one morning. I remember the dew-wet grass on my shoes. I remember Daddy leading the way up a hill. I remember the forms of others there growing clearer in the fleeting darkness. And then, I remember voices as deep as the first line: "Low in the grave he lay . . . waiting the coming day." Then there was a little pause, like the disciples lingering at Jesus's tomb, staring at the death of all their dreams. Then with voices that from the first word seemed to rise along with Christ, we sang, "Up from the grave he arose! . . . Hallelujah! Christ arose!" We picked up from that hymn to Bliss's Easter portrait of the "Man of Sorrows."

> Lifted up was he to die;
> It is finished was his cry;
> Now in heaven exalted high.
> Hallelujah! What a Saviour![6]

Cheryl Beckett

I'll never forget that first Easter sunrise service and its opening praises, and I can never get away from that pause between the grave and glory. It is the place of unanswered questions, and I've had a lot of those lately. I got a call from Afghanistan early one morning in August and learned that my friend Cheryl Beckett had been killed, along with nine other aid workers. They were ambushed by Islamic militants. I can't allow myself to even think about how she died. She was a beautiful soul who never failed to lift my spirits with her joy in Christ. Our time together in June was precious—although at the time, I didn't know just how precious. I don't expect a good answer to why at thirty-two-years of age she should be taken. She brought so much strength to the team, and she put Calvary love on display for the Afghan people to see. There are already so few there, so few willing to go there. It still hurts to write about her.

MADISON, OHIO

Staying a couple of miles from Lake Erie. The house is quiet and sleep beckons, but this has been a day to remember. Took a walk with Chris and Joe up from the ball field to the old trestle, where long ago Bliss and his wife lost their lives. We walked through autumn splendor. Leaves, which screened the westering sun, looked like stained glass set in a cathedral of trees that scattered colorful confetti in our way. As we walked, Joe told us about Bliss, who was one of the most popular and influential musicians of his time. Bliss coined the term "Gospel song," and his partnership with D. L. Moody and fellow hymn writer Ira Sankey spread his ministry to both sides of the Atlantic. Just before Christmas 1876, Moody was preaching in Chicago to thousands daily. At that time Bliss was engaged in evangelistic meetings in the Midwest, but Moody asked him to come to Chicago and help. Bliss returned home to Pennsylvania to spend Christmas with his family, and then he and Lucy left their young sons in the care of Bliss's mother and sister and set out for Chicago. The evening of December 29, the train pushed through northeastern Ohio in a blizzard. As it crossed the Ashtabula River, the trestle cracked and gave way, plunging all the passenger cars seventy feet down into the river. Kerosene stoves inside the wooden rail cars spread fire rapidly through the crash. Philip and Lucy died along with ninety-two others, their remains completely consumed by the fire. Bliss was thirty-eight years old.

We stood near that rebuilt trestle. The river mirrored nothing but a peaceful afternoon. The sound of a passing train was the only reminder of the carnage that once lay here. So we sang Bliss's tunes, "It Is Well with My Soul" and "Hallelujah! What a Saviour."

Joe told me that Bliss had sent his luggage to Chicago ahead of them, and his suitcases arrived before the news of his death. A friend opened the luggage and found the lines of a new hymn Bliss was working on.

> I know not what awaits me,
> God kindly veils my eyes,
> And o'er each step of my onward way,
> He makes new scenes to rise;
> And ev'ry joy he sends me comes,
> A sweet and glad surprise,

So on I go, not knowing,
I would not if I might;
I'd rather walk in the dark with God,
Than go alone in the light;
I'd rather walk by faith with him,
Than go alone by sight.[7]

"So on I go not knowing . . . I'd rather walk in the dark with God"—I was stunned. I immediately thought of Cheryl Beckett's last letter to us this summer. She included this poem:

I see your hands,
not white and manicured
but scarred and scratched and competent,
reach out
not always to remove the weight I carry
but to shift its balance, ease it,
make it bearable.
Lord, if this is where you want me,
I'm content.
No, not quite true. I wish it were.
All I can say, in honesty is this.
If this is where I'm meant to be
I'll stay. And try.
Just let me feel your hands.[8]

He being dead, she being dead, "yet speaketh" (Heb. 11:4 KJV). Bliss and Beckett, they're both reminding me that Christ has not promised answers to all our sorrows. All he has ever really promised is his presence—and that is enough.

BABYLON, IRAQ

Set out for Iraq from Abu Dhabi. The glittering Emirates are like a high-rise mirage shimmering above the Arabian sandflats, but the mirage soon disappeared into the unbounded blueness of the Persian Gulf as our plane turned northward toward Iraq. The plane was filled with its own Babel of tongues—Mandarin, Russian,

Dutch, Korean, Turkish, Arabic, and English—businessmen bound for Baghdad in search of gold. My friend Jason and I are here looking for opportunity, too—gospel opportunity.

Arrived in Baghdad about noon and immediately set off for Hillah and the ruins of Babylon. Took the highway south of Baghdad, which is grimly known as the "Road of Death" because of all the victims of IEDs and suicide bombers which have been claimed along this stretch. The bomb-twisted wreckage of cars and trucks marked the way.

Reached Babylon midafternoon. Only the biblical accounts and the ancient chroniclers can resurrect from the current heaps of dust and mud bricks the splendor of a place whose very name means the "Garden of God." Intriguing, since Genesis records that one of the rivers that flowed from Eden was the Euphrates, which still snakes through the remains of this once-great city.

I walked where Daniel walked as I crossed the Procession Street built by Nebuchadnezzar and entered the excavated and rebuilt portion of the royal palace, including the throne room. Likely, Daniel stood before the king here and interpreted his dreams and told of things yet to come. One brick stamped in spindly cuneiform characters twenty-six centuries ago noted that these great walls were raised by Nebuchadnezzar! Could it be in this very room that another hand wrote on this wall in the time of Belshazzar, and these very stones echoed with the voice of Daniel reading the divine sentence: "You have been weighed in the balances and found wanting" (Dan. 5:27)?

I climbed up the side of the old moat in the unexcavated part for a better view. Somewhere in the shadow of these ruins stood Nebuchadnezzar's golden idol, along with Shadrach, Meshach, and Abednego, who also stood—unbowed. Here Daniel spent a quiet night with lions. This is a Hebrews 11 place, where men through faith "stopped the mouths of lions, quenched the power of fire" (Heb. 11:33–34).

I found an even more commanding view of the ruins of Babylon from the palace of Saddam Hussein, who chose this site overlooking Babylon and the Euphrates because he prided himself as a second Nebuchadnezzar. The palace is now empty and looted, its stripped walls gilded only with graffiti. Soldiers have nailed a basketball hoop to the wall of Saddam's throne room so now it's just a place to shoot free throws, to dance on his grave.

The sun now drifts beyond the Euphrates, and the first stars appear. It will be a long, late drive back to Baghdad.

BAGHDAD, IRAQ

Set out this morning for the three-hour drive south toward Nasiriyah. For security reasons, and to avoid that Shiite hotbed, we went quietly around the plains of Ur. From a great distance, we could see the ziggurat that was the centerpiece of this city of Abraham. Our Iraqi guide was named Dhaiph. His grandfather had worked with the British expedition that excavated part of Ur in the 1920s and 1930s, but much of Ur's mysteries still remain beneath the barren plains. Only a scattering of mounds mark the places where tantalizing treasure has yet to be unearthed.

Climbed the ziggurat to find the best view of Ur. In the distance, Blackhawk helicopters were on patrol. They swept in and then turned just above us, a jarring juxtaposition to the four-thousand-year-old landmark. Afterward we went down into the royal tombs of Ur-Nammu, who was likely the king when Abraham and Sarah lived here. A staircase led deep into the ground into a great brick vault tomb that still had timbers that British archaeologists had propped it up with eighty years ago. The floor was spongy, carpeted by centuries of accumulated dust and bird dung. Ur-Nammu oversaw an urban culture that produced a writing system, made practical use of the wheel, and developed a mathematics system based on the number sixty, which we still use on our clocks and compasses. By their engineering and creative energy, these ancient people produced a city with paved roads, sewer systems, impressive

230

temples, and the world's earliest museum. In short, Abraham and Sarah's lives were cultured, comfortable, and cluttered with idols.

But then, something unexpected happened here that changed everything. God—the only *real* God—revealed himself to Abraham and called him to leave Ur and all its wonders and familiar things and "by faith Abraham obeyed when he was called to go out to a place that he was to receive as an inheritance. And he went out, not knowing where he was going" (Heb. 11:8). A certain righteous restlessness settled in Abraham's heart, as he never really felt at home again until he reached another "city that has foundations, whose designer and builder is God" (11:10). That journey began here. The crunch of pottery shards beneath my feet, the wind-driven dust over the emptiness, makes it all so real today.

SOMEWHERE IN BAGHDAD, EAST OF THE TIGRIS

This morning we were stopped at an Iraqi Army checkpoint southeast of Baghdad. After some questioning, we were taken to a second checkpoint, where our passports were confiscated, and we were detained for a time. Afterward, we were escorted by Iraqi forces to an Iraqi Army post, where Jason and I were photographed and questioned at length. No explanation has been offered as to why we were being held. The Iraqi officer in charge reported that we were to be sent to the brigade headquarters to see General Abdul Azeeri. So we were separated from our interpreter and taken under armed guard to an Iraqi base called Alrusafa. I'm now in the office of the deputy commander, and between questions I'm using this time to write. The Iraqi colonel is sitting behind a desk of polished walnut with neat stacks that an aide keeps tidied up for the great man. His shoulders are weighed down by the gold-crested epaulets of power, and a big pistol holster circles his considerable girth. The commander's jutting jaw and penchant for thumping the desk as he talks to us reminds me of an old Mussolini newsreel. Not sure when we're getting out of here, or even why we're being held, or if we will miss our flight tomorrow. Still have my Blackberry, though.

When the sun was setting a couple of hours ago and the last *azan* was sounding from mosques all over Baghdad, I sent a quick message to Debbie to send out our own "call to prayer." I'm confident, though, that ours will have results.

CAMP VICTORY, BAGHDAD

Blackhawks are humming overhead, as the sun brightens the sky east of the Tigris. These past twenty-four hours have been unforgettable—a reminder that our King commands generals and spies and also guides the steps of his children. Angels come in many forms. Last night mine came in the form of a Skoal-spitting army colonel from Alabama. After nearly ten hours in the custody of the Iraqi Army, suddenly Colonel Cole with the 82nd Airborne arrived and sought to take custody of us. It seems that a few hours earlier we had been spotted by his Kurdish interpreter, who had reported to him that he thought he saw some Americans with Iraqi troops.

After some back and forth, Jason and I were able to go with Cole, but we were not allowed to leave the Iraqi base. As it turned out, we ended up at the U.S. Army's last outpost east of the Tigris River. Although the details are classified, what the colonel could tell me was that Iranian-backed groups were looking for American targets to kill or kidnap, especially before the upcoming United States troop withdrawal. Elements in the Iraqi Army were providing these groups with intelligence, and it looks as if we were in their sights.

The Army Rangers then went to work on a plan to move us to the airport. So at 2:30 a.m. we strapped on vests and helmets and set out in a convoy of three MRAPs, crossed the Tigris River, and went on to the airbase here at Camp Victory. Have just been briefed by several Air Force undercover agents who have laid out a plan for maneuvering Jason and me past the checkpoints outside and inside the Baghdad airport. We set out soon for this last round of cat-and-mouse—and hopefully our flight back to Abu Dhabi!

It seems my idea of a tour company in Baghdad may be a little premature, but there must be other ways to position Christians here

232

for the sake of the gospel. All these businessmen I flew in with four days ago are still here—risking their resources and even their lives in order to make money. Why can't Christians risk at least as much for the gospel?

Daniel in his time risked everything in this land to spread the fame of his God. He kept company with lions and angels and proclaimed the King of kings. Lord, send another Daniel here. Call more Abrahams and Sarahs to leave the things that will turn to dust anyway to make your glory and your gospel known.

EPILOGUE

The dogwoods outside my window are coming to life in the early spring air. Soon I'll see long stretches of desert and razor wire, but this morning it's good to be home and write, to mix ink with coffee. Murphy the Cat is overseeing my work here in my study. He, too, dreams of adventures. At times, I think I've seen him leading leopards on a hunt deep in the Serengeti. The pack moves swift and silent, limb to limb, flying fur and fang. Murphy's green eyes widen and whiskers twitch at the thought of it—just before slipping into another nap on his perch on the windowsill. I think he has some Walter Mitty in him.

My study walls are lined with books, swords, and portraits of the soldiers among my ancestors. A battle-scarred German helmet props up a stack of my old journals and a sheaf of worn maps. Above, there is a display of medals. My favorites are the British war medals given by the Crown, sterling stamped with the image of the king or queen, along with the name of the soldier.

On the front lines of gospel advance, there are no medals, no helmets or swords—just men and women transformed and driven by the gospel to take the message of Christ to the next city or country or next door. By their lives and witness, they magnify the greatness of their Captain, the certainty of his victory, and his surpassing grace that makes the weak strong. And like these medals, my fellow soldiers bear the image of their King.

But this long campaign—this hard, happy work—won't be done until our Captain calls us to himself. And so for my part, I am preparing to step through the long passageway again that leads to my sisters and brothers on the other side of the ocean. They are a gospel force, and there will be amazing kingdom stories to tell, for the wind of the Spirit is sweeping over lands that have for too long had "impossible" written over them. I recall what Zwemer said of those hard places:

> The kingdoms and the governments of this world have frontiers which must not be crossed, but the Gospel of Jesus Christ knows no frontier. It has never been kept within bounds. It is a message for the whole race, and the very fact that there are millions of souls who have never heard the message becomes the strongest of reasons why we must carry it to them. Every year we hear of further advance into these regions of the world by commerce, by travelers, and by men of science. If they can open a way for themselves, in spite of all these difficulties, shall the ambassadors of the cross shrink back? God can open doors. He is "the Great Opener." He opens the lips of the dumb to song, the eyes of the blind to sight, and the prison house to the captive. He opens the doors of utterance and entrance of the Gospel. He opens graves and gates, the windows of heaven and the bars of death. He holds all the keys of every situation.[1]

As I prepare for my next journey with its obstacles, I find myself echoing the words of the women on resurrection morning: "'Who will roll away the stone for us from the entrance of the tomb?' And looking up, they saw that the stone had been rolled back—it was very large" (Mark 16:3–4). Lord Jesus, the stone before me is also beyond my strength. Cause me to look up, open the way, fling aside the stone again, that we may see your glory.

NOTES

Prologue
1. David Nichols, ed., *Ernie's War: The Best of Ernie Pyle's World War II Dispatches* (New York: Random House, 1986), 113.

Chapter 1: End of Empire
1. Tim Keesee, ed., "Prison Song," *The Messenger*, Spring 2006 (Frontline Missions International: 2006), 1.
2. *The King and His Hawk*, retold by James Baldwin, in *The Book of Virtues: A Treasury of Great Moral Stories*, ed. William Bennett (New York: Simon & Schuster, 1993), 37–39.
3. Percy Bysshe Shelley, "Ozymandias," in *The Norton Anthology of English Literature, 7th ed.*, ed. M. H. Abrams (New York: W. W. Norton, 2000), 2:726.

Chapter 2: Children of Cain
1. Rebecca West, *Black Lamb and Grey Falcon* (New York: Penguin, 1984), 54–55.
2. David continued to share Christ with Nikoll by letter, his sense of urgency heightened by the fact that Nikoll was suffering from a terminal lung disease. Theresa hand-delivered David's letters, and shortly before Nikoll died, he wrote David the following: "I received your letter with great joy. . . . I believe on Jesus and your words about the resurrection. Even though I am a poor man, I see you are just like me. Even though I am sick, you have healed me with your letter. We love Jesus as He loves us. . . . I will return my whole life and family to Jesus Christ and my biggest gift will be to be a Christian in every place I work. I will be the most devoted worker of your church and above all of Jesus Christ, until the very end." Printed in Frontline Missions International's newsletter *Dispatches* (Fall 2011): 3.
3. C. S. Lewis, *The Lion, the Witch, and the Wardrobe* (New York: Harper, 2000), 106.

Chapter 3: Ten Sparrows
1. Quoted in John Franklin Goucher, *Growth of the Missionary Concept* (New York: Eaton & Mains, 1911), 21.

2. Craig Brian Larson and Brian Lowery, *1001 Quotations That Connect: Timeless Wisdom for Preaching, Teaching, and Writing* (Grand Rapids, MI: Zondervan, 2009), 101.
3. Quoted in *Our Daily Bread*, May 13, 1996.
4. Roger Steer, *J. Hudson Taylor: A Man in Christ* (Wheaton, IL: Harold Shaw, 1990), 172.
5. Ibid., 173.
6. Ibid., 174.
7. A. J. Broomhall, *Hudson Taylor and China's Open Century*, bk. 5, *Refiner's Fire* (London: Hodder and Stoughton and Overseas Missionary Fellowship, 1985), 373.

Chapter 4: Within a Yard of Hell
1. Letter to Tim Keesee, originally published in "Sudden Joy," *The Messenger*, Winter 2007 (Frontline Missions International), 1.
2. Norman P. Grubb, *C. T. Studd: Cricketer & Pioneer* (Fort Washington, PA: CLC Publications, 2008), 145.
3. Robert D. Kaplan, *The Ends of the Earth: A Journey at the Dawn of the 21st Century* (New York: Random House, 1996), 419–20.
4. Anonymous, "The Power of His Rising" (harmonization copyright, Fred and Ruth Coleman, 2013).

Chapter 5: Souls of the Brave
1. Isaac Watts and Bob Kauflin, "Alas, and Did My Savior Bleed," *Songs for the Cross Centered Life* (Sovereign Grace Praise, 1997), www.sovereign gracemusic.org.
2. Mark Twain, *Following the Equator: A Journey around the World* (New York: Harper & Brothers, 1897), 300.
3. Ibid., 301.
4. Arthur Hugh Clough, *Amours de Voyage*, canto 5, part 6, lines 5–6.
5. Attributed to S. Sundar Singh, "Assam," Hindustani melody.

Chapter 6: Amazing Grace
1. Marlise Simons and J. David Goodman, "Ex-Liberian Leader Gets 50 Years for War Crimes," *New York Times*, May 30, 2012.
2. Leslie T. Lyall, *A Passion for the Impossible: The Continuing Story of the Mission Hudson Taylor Began* (London: OMF Books, 1965), 98.

Chapter 7: Prison Break
1. A. Katherine Hankey, "I Love to Tell the Story," *Praise and Worship: The Nazarene Hymnal* (Kansas City: Nazarene Publishing House, 1951), no. 223.
2. Lawrence Wright, *The Looming Tower: Al-Qaeda and the Road to 9/11* (New York: Alfred A. Knopf, 2006), 166–67.

3. Rupert Brooke, "The Soldier," in *The Norton Anthology of English Literature: The Twentieth Century and After*, ed. Stephen Greenblatt (New York: W. W. Norton, 2006), F:1955–56.

Chapter 8: Dimmed by Dust
1. Samuel M. Zwemer, "The Glory of the Impossible," in *The Unoccupied Mission Fields of Africa and Asia* (New York: Student Volunteer Movement for Foreign Missions, 1911), 218.
2. Stanislaw Baranczak, "If China," in *Against Forgetting: Twentieth-Century Poetry of Witness*, ed. Carolyn Forche (New York: W. W. Norton, 1993), 480.
3. Graham Kendrick, "Knowing You," Make Way Music, 1993, www.grahamkendrick.co.uk.
4. John Kent, "Sovereign Grace O'er Sin Abounding," *A New Selection of Seven Hundred Evangelical Hymns*, ed. John Dobell (Morristown, NJ: Peter A. Johnson, 1810), no. 634.
5. Samuel M. Zwemer and Amy E. Zwemer, *Topsy-Turvy Land: Arabia Pictured for Children* (New York: Revell, 1902), 116.
6. Philip P. Bliss, "Hallelujah! What a Savior!," 1875.
7. Mary G. Brainard, arr. Philip P. Bliss, "He Knows," 1876.
8. Eddie Askew, "I See Your Hands," in *Many Voices, One Voice: Meditations and Prayers* (Petersborough, UK: The Leprosy Mission International, 1985), 39.

Epilogue
1. Samuel M. Zwemer, *The Unoccupied Mission Fields of Africa and Asia* (New York: Student Volunteer Movement for Foreign Missions, 1911), 90.

DISPATCHES FROM THE FRONT
DVD SERIES

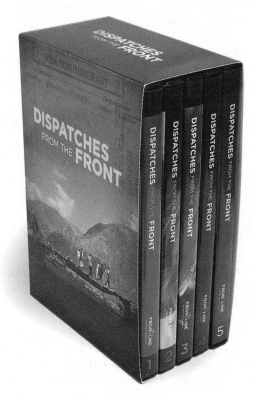

Dispatches from the Front is an ongoing documentary series that opens windows to the advance of Christ's kingdom all around the world, showcasing the gospel's unstoppable power. This DVD series highlights the marvelous extent, diversity, and unity of the church. The journal format of each episode underscores the unfolding of God's activity on the "front lines," bringing viewers up close to the sights and sounds of Christians from distant corners of the kingdom.

"The narrative is as beautifully crafted as the stories are inspiring."
JOHN PIPER, *Founder, desiringGod.org*

"I want, and I want my kids to have, a heart for world missions. These videos stir that passion. . . . I would highly recommend this series."
JOSHUA HARRIS, *Senior Pastor, Covenant Life Church*

To view trailers, videos clips, and to order, visit dispatchesfromthefront.org.
Also available at wtsbooks.com and amazon.com.